The Anarchist's Arms

THE YEAR IS 2020, and London - the capital of Europe - teeters on the edge of a general conflagration, while a million demonstrators take to the streets in a kaleidoscope of focus groups

Errol Flynt, the newly re-elected Mayor, looks on in quiet despair, and delegates ambitious Robert Greene, ace-pamphleteer and Deputy-Deputy Mayor - on his afternoon off - to enter the fray as observer.

On Fleet Street, hydrogen-powered vehicles form the greatest traffic jam in history.

At The Arms, Robert Greene takes up - or avoids - the issues with the tavern's guests . . .Among a cast of thousands, enter . . .Horace Baker, long-serving retainer, amateur rebel and suspected arsonist . . .George Foxxe, last proprietor of The Arms, who has been drugged up to his eyeballs by his new "wife" on behalf of the greedy Conglomerate . . .Mr Shine, the ghostly tour guide whose circular tour never ends . . .and Elaine Wichell, student of the paranormal, who sees "layers", and acts as companion to Margaret Foxxe, George's powerful sister over from Manhattan to sniff out assets. . . .Enter Stage Extreme Right: the Ancient Order of Frothblowers, a group of businessmen on the town, who are worse, Margaret Foxxe says, than "the thugs".

Socialist or socialite, anarchist or arsonist, merchant banker or beggar, lawyer or ghost, all are welcome - or not - at *THE ANARCHIST'S ARMS*. . . - A political comedy to agitate every part of the spectrum - and beyond. . .

By the same author:

NOVEL
A Footprint in the Sand

NON-FICTION
The Bering Strait Project: Symposium (Editor)

James A. Oliver is an international writer, editor, and journalist. He is also the author of A *Footprint in the Sand* - a political comedy inspired by a "special assignment" at the end of the Cold War. . . James Oliver is currently working on a non-fiction title *The Bering Strait Crossing: A 21st Century Frontier* - which is being translated into several languages for release in 2005.

The
Anarchist's
Arms

A Political Comedy in Three Acts for the Stage

James A. Oliver

The COMPANY of WRITERS

First Published in the United Kingdom 2004
by The Company of Writers
www.thecompanyofwriters.com

© 2004 James A. Oliver

James A. Oliver has asserted his right under the Copyright,
Designs and Patents Act 1988.

ISBN 0-9546995-5-6

British Library Cataloguing in Publication Data.
A catalogue record for this book is available from the British Library.

D R A M A T I S   P E R S O N Æ

HORACE BAKER
A long-time retainer of *The Arms*, bartender, waiter, and general assistant.

ROBERT GREENE
Deputy-Deputy Mayor and ace pamphleteer.

ERROL FLYNT
Mayor of London (re-elected).

JAMES BEAM
Professor attached to Columbia University; specialist in crowd dynamics; on a field trip to London.

GEORGE FOXXE
Anglo-American, wheelchair-bound owner of *The Arms*.

BARBARA:
New "wife" to George Foxxe; acting manageress of *The Arms*, she is an undercover operative of the Conglomerate in its clandestine take-over attempt.

MARGARET FOXXE
A powerful New York City dowager socialite, she is George Foxxe's younger sister; visiting London at the start of a European tour.

ELAINE WICHELL
Companion to Margaret Foxxe; student of the paranormal.

CARLTON GREY
Merchant banker, advisor to Margaret Foxxe, vet (special forces).

MR SHINE
Tour guide in a red-blazer, whose circular journey never ends.

A GROUP *of* TOURISTS: Mr Shine's flock, which includes: MISS ASHE, MR STOKER, and EVA FOXXE (the first MRS FOXXE) ~ all deceased. THE ANCIENT ORDER OF FROTHBLOWERS, an unruly group of five businessmen; on the town for their annual bash. JEFFREY & PHYLLIS CAMERON, a couple on their (second) honeymoon. BAKUNIN, THE WILD MAN, in a grey trenchcoat; a pin-striped LAWYER, a portly MERCHANT BANKER, and DR SAXXE-COBURG, a scientist; MISS PERKINS, Deeply Personal Assistant to the MAYOR. RIOTERS & assorted DEMONSTRATORS belonging to a multitude of focus groups; a female RED-HEAD with a placard; a COURIER; two DETECTIVES.

THE PROLOGUE

Dark. Curtains remain closed. A spotlight hits the curtain to reveal MAYOR ERROL FLYNT in a skillful embrace with MISS PERKINS - a pensive brunette. The scene is a notional view of the Mayor's Office. ERROL FLYNT wears a slick Italian sharkskin suite. They part.

ERROL FLYNT: Excellent, Miss Perkins. Excellent! Progress - that's what I like to see. How I love this City!

MISS PERKINS: Why, thank you, Errol. [*Frowns*]: Ah, Mr Mayor.

ERROL FLYNT: Excellent, Miss Perkins! [*Thumbs hooked into trouser-waistband*]: Now, who did you say that was on the 'phone? [*Looks into the upstage distance.*]

MISS PERKINS (*wipes her brow*): Your counterpart in New York.

ERROL FLYNT (*teasingly*): My counterpart in New York have a name?

MISS PERKINS (*flushes*): Mayor Gambini?

ERROL FLYNT: That's him, all right. [*Looks at her with fresh eyes; she takes a half-step away.*] Well, Miss Perkins, what does Mayor Gambini have to say for himself?

MISS PERKINS: He sends his congratulations on your re-election victory, sir.

ERROL FLYNT (*smiles, modestly*): Anything else?

MISS PERKINS: The riots in New York last year? [*The spotlight wavers, then steadies.*]

ERROL FLYNT (*his eyes flicker*): Riots . . .? What about the riots?

MISS PERKINS: Mayor Gambini says they may have made an identification. A suspect. One of the agitators. A possible ringleader. A man in a blue suit. The photography is grainy -

but they're working on an enhancement right now. They'll send it through on SkyNet when it's ready.

ERROL FLYNT: An enhancement? [*Almost leers at her.*] Well, that's excellent, Miss Perkins. But - is any of this relevant?

MISS PERKINS: Relevant? Oh sure: they think he's headed this way; or that he is already here.

ERROL FLYNT: The Network?

MISS PERKINS: Not the Network. Freelance, they think.

ERROL FLYNT: Freelance? Extraordinary. You're very well informed, Miss Perkins. Dangerous?

MISS PERKINS: Who, me? Oh, I thought you meant -. Indirectly, Errol.

ERROL FLYNT (*sighs*): Indirectly Errol? Interesting. Well, we'll flush out our man soon, then.

MISS PERKINS: They've sent an agent. An observer. Covert, I believe. An academic.

ERROL FLYNT: An academic? In a situation like this?

MISS PERKINS: A professor of some kind.

ERROL FLYNT: That's a real Gambini touch. [*Checks his wristwatch.*] Now, where were we?

MISS PERKINS: We were . . .discussing my promotion.

ERROL FLYNT: Is *that* what we were doing?

MISS PERKINS: Yes, Mr Mayor, we certainly were!

ERROL FLYNT (*turns his back on her*): How would you like to be a Deputy to the Deputy Major, Miss Perkins? It's a direct appointment. In other words, it's in my gift

MISS PERKINS (*elated*): You mean - I don't have to run for election?

ERROL FLYNT: No. [*Quietly*]: You only have to . . .

MISS PERKINS: Well, how many deputy-deputies are there, Errol?

ERROL FLYNT (*turns on her*): What did you say?

MISS PERKINS: I said - yes, I'd like that very much.

ERROL FLYNT: The position is occupied at the moment, but not for long. The London Assembly Way: Up, and then Out. [*Uses his right hand to show promotion, then ejection from the top floor*.] Now, in the meantime, I want you to reach Mayor Gambini on the telephone.

MISS PERKINS: Yes, Mr Mayor! Right away! [*Moves Stage R.*] On your way out, show in Bob Greene.

MISS PERKINS: Yes, Mr Mayor!

> [*ERROL FLYNT waits Centre-Stage; he smiles, deeply amused. Enter Stage R. ROBERT GREENE - in an electric-blue suit.*]

ROBERT GREENE: You wanted to see me, Errol?

ERROL FLYNT (*grins*): You've done a great job, Bob. [*They shake hands, but keep their distance*.] Ten-out-of-ten for effort.

ROBERT GREENE: Why, thank you, Errol.

ERROL FLYNT: - And one out of ten for achievement.

ROBERT GREENE: Oh.

ERROL FLYNT (*with a grin*): Just kidding, Bob. That's one of Mayor Gambini's wisecracks. Thought I'd try it out.

ROBERT GREENE: Sure. Now I recall. The New York delegation last year.

ERROL FLYNT: We had a great time, didn't we? [*ROBERT GREENE does not respond.*] Seriously, Bob, you've done a great job. Great copy. Great pamphlets. You don't regret leaving the ad agency to join my campaign? The promotion ladder can be pretty frustrating in the public sector. You know, some people feel they don't get on as fast as they *think* they deserve.

ROBERT GREENE: The public sector is where I belong, Errol. What could be more worthwhile than serving the public? [*Leers upstage.*]

ERROL FLYNT: What, indeed? Well, now that I've been re-elected, it's my policy to advance new talent.

ROBERT GREENE: You ran a great campaign, Mr Mayor.

ERROL FLYNT: Sure I did. With your help. . .I'm confident your promotion will come through any day now. Deputy Mayor: how does that sound? No more of this deputy-deputy business; it's humiliating, that's what it is. I wonder which idiot came up with that one? [*Realises it is himself.*]

ROBERT GREENE: I wouldn't like to say - Errol.

ERROL FLYNT (*looks at his feet*): Don't say anything; just say yes, and take the rest of the day off. See how things are at ground level. I mean, we can't have the Assembly executive losing its perspective, can we? I'd go with you, but on a day like today, they'd probably hang me out to dry. [*Seems to peer outside.*] Nice day for it, too. This is what Mrs Flynt used to call 'good drying weather'.

ROBERT GREENE: Mrs Flynt?

ERROL FLYNT (*looks up*): There's trouble brewing, Bob. I've got to know that I can depend on you.

ROBERT GREENE: You can; you can.

ERROL FLYNT: I'm surrounded by Yes-men and Yes-Women; I can't depend on them. I need people who can say "No" to me.

ROBERT GREENE: In that case, I'd rather not take the afternoon off, Errol.

ERROL FLYNT: You're to take the afternoon off. The London Eye has detected a disturbance in the City. If you should happen to stroll along Fleet Street, I want you to take a look around. Understand?

ROBERT GREENE: I'm not sure I do.

ERROL FLYNT: You can observe, but not in any official capacity. You're my eyes and ears, but not officially. Try The Arms. [*Folds his arms.*] George Foxxe runs it; a strange kind of a place. Haunted, they say.

ROBERT GREENE: Yes, I think I know the establishment.

ERROL FLYNT: Corporate Affairs is looking into it, but not officially. You can, on your afternoon off, base your observations from there . . .One more thing.

ROBERT GREENE: Yes?

ERROL FLYNT: On your way out, send in Miss Perkins. I haven't finished with her yet.

ROBERT GREENE: Yes, Mr Mayor. [*Turns to leave.*]

MAJOR FLYNT: Remember: don't say yes to me, Bob.

ROBERT GREENE: *No*, Mr Mayor. [*Departs.*]

> [*The spotlight contracts to show ERROL FLYNT's election-winning smile. In the off-stage distance, the crowd roars its defiance. Spotlight to dark.*]

ACT I

In the near future, London - the capital of Europe - is on the verge of a general conflagration. . .In the streets of the City, the demonstration has not yet turned to riot. The action is centred on an old tavern in Fleet Street. The set is the first-floor lounge area of The Arms. . . A long oak table is positioned downstage beneath an observation window. . . Tables, chairs, a fish in a glass case, maps, portraits of obscure personages, etc. ~ a cubicle for four people at Stage L. At Stage R., a snug bar is positioned downstage. Behind the bar, a dumb waiter is set into the wall. Either side of the dumb waiter, shelves - wine, spirits, liqueurs. On the bar, a couple of hand-pulled beerpumps point at the ceiling. At extreme Stage R. an archway leads onto a stairwell void. A carpet - a red runner - stretches between the void and a portal at extreme Stage L.

Beyond the observation window, the dome of St Paul's Cathedral flickers into existence. It is neither day or night, dusk nor dawn. Outside, the greatest, hydrogen-powered traffic jam in history comes to a grinding halt.

THE ENVOY

Curtains. No lights. Dim spotlight appears Centre-Stage. Enter Stage L. portal BAKUNIN, THE WILD MAN, in a grey trenchcoat and riding boots. In his left hand, he carries a torch of flame. Beneath a shock of grey hair, his eyes bulge. On a long chain, he pulls out a handsome pocket watch, then replaces the timepiece. On time, he strides upstage.

BAKUNIN: So, it has begun. There is a conflagration all over Europe - and beyond. And I . . .I thought I was LOST TO THE WORLD! I know the time, all right, but what year is this. . ? 1848? 1968?. . .20-something? [*Looks over his shoulder, downstage, at Saint Paul's in the distance . . .Turns, looks upstage at us with a smile of relish.*]

And they said it could never happen here!

[*There are shouts in the distance.*]

Well, we'll see about that, comrades! Are you ready to go the distance?

[*Raises his bushy eyebrows.*] Begin! Begin, I say!

[*Turns with a swirl of his trenchcoat, and storms off towards Stage R., where he takes a running vault along the crimson carpet - and plunges through the archway void. Silence.*]

SCENE ONE

Fade-in lights. It is about mid-day. Outside, there is a steady, hypnotic hum of traffic, and then the stream of vehicles, encountering some unseen blockade, comes to a halt: there are shouts, whistles and honks, which coalesce into general mayhem [Fade away, gradually.] Inside the tavern, a tranquility from the horse-drawn era pervades. In the distance, a riot is in progress. There is a recognisable shout of "Capitalist scum!" Then: "Who are you calling scum, SCUM!

JAMES BEAM is seated at a Centre-Stage table. He smokes a cigar and reads alarming headlines from a newspaper. . . Guests stand around the snug bar: the CAMERONS, DR SAXXE~COBURG, a pin-striped LAWYER, and a portly MERCHANT BANKER. At Stage R., a blue-suited ROBERT GREENE appears at the archway void. Outside, a frenzied crowd seems to greet his arrival. He pauses - then approaches the snug bar, and motions at HORACE for a glass of beer.

LAWYER: So much for the Mayor's anti-congestion policy.

MERCHANT BANKER: So much for *any* of his polices.

LAWYER: He started out as a bus conductor, you know.

MERCHANT BANKER: And finished up as Mayor? I did not know. Surely you jest?

[*ROBERT GREENE almost splutters into his beer glass.*]

LAWYER: I jest not. And that's not all: years ago, his father was knocked down by a bus on Christmas Eve.

MERCHANT BANKER: Whose father?

LAWYER: Why, Errol Flynt's father, of course.

MERCHANT: You mean, he has a father?

LAWYER: For a merchant banker, you don't know much worth knowing.

MERCHANT: For a lawyer, you seem to know everything.

LAWYER: For instance: guess who the conductor was on that very same bus?

MERCHANT BANKER: The youthful Flynt? The son?

LAWYER: Seems he never got over it. The source, they say, of his motivation - all that ambition.

MERCHANT BANKER: Guilt . . ?

LAWYER: No, transport.

[*The two men collude.*]

PHYLLIS CAMERON (*looks downstage*): Look - the sun - it's disappeared! Jeffrey - it's . . .gone.

JEFFREY CAMERON: Please, Phyllis, let's not start all of that again.

MERCHANT BANKER: Is that possible - at midday?

DR SAXXE-COBURG: The next eclipse is not due until, until-.

LAWYER: This building is said to possess many unusual aspects. A strange case indeed. The River Fleet runs beneath our feet - down into the Thames.

DR SAXXE-COBURG: Magnetic resonance, that kind of thing?

LAWYER (*leans*): I'm inclined to speak here of a strange topography, Herr Doctor.

[*They continue to talk among themselves. The LAWYER puts a silent question to HORACE, who denies all knowledge, while studying the planks beneath his feet. . .BARBARA appears at Stage R. JAMES BEAM looks up, only half-surprised, as she approaches his table.*]

BARBARA: Expecting someone else, Professor Beam? [*She stands by his table.*]

JAMES BEAM: I was expecting your husband George, Mrs Foxxe. Yesterday and today, he's missed our game of cards.

BARBARA: It's true, he did enjoy your talks together. He told me as much during *our* talks together. But he's a married man again, Professor, and there are so many pressing matters to deal with here at The Arms.

JAMES BEAM: Where is-?

BARBARA (*looks up at the ceiling*): -He's in his studio now. He's being oiled this afternoon.

JAMES BEAM: Oiled? You're kidding, right?

BARBARA: I never *kid*, Professor Beam. [*Listens.*] That's him now.

> [*The sound of a freshly oiled wheelchair moves jauntily back and forth across the floor above the ceiling.*]

I hope he doesn't injure himself.

JAMES BEAM: Surely, he's *already* injured himself?

BARBARA: Oh, no, he's resting. Thank you for your concern, Professor, but he's only *resting* in the wheelchair. He's tired, dead tired. After so many years on his feet, why not indeed?

JAMES BEAM: I take it he's still the proprietor of this establishment?

BARBARA: What a bizarre question, Professor. Still, you're tired, too, aren't you? After your trip across the Atlantic: jet lag?

JAMES BEAM: I'm getting over it.

BARBARA: Anyway, Professor Beam, you'll be seeing George soon enough. He's making a surprise announcement: he's decided to have his birthday three days' early. Everyone is invited down to the riverboat for luncheon.

JAMES BEAM: So much for the surprise announcement.

BARBARA: I'm still trying to talk him out of it, but - well, I never realised until today what . . .enormous will power he-. Well, enough said. Except-.

JAMES BEAM: Except what, Mrs Foxxe?

BARBARA: It's unlikely he'll be able to join us.

JAMES BEAM: On his own birthday?

BARBARA: He's as woozy as can be - with sleep. He says we're to go on ahead without him, while he rests in his studio.

[*Above the ceiling, the wheelchair - creak-creak-creak - seems eager.*]

JAMES BEAM: Sounds like he's trying to get out of there.

BARBARA (*ignores the remark*): It's so very complicated, you see: we have a group booking here at The Arms for this very evening. Under the circumstances, I thought they might have cancelled, or perhaps they simply won't show. . .[*Smiles*]: Anyway, I would appreciate your discretion.

JAMES BEAM: About what exactly?

BARBARA: I don't know why I'm telling you this, really.

JAMES BEAM: I was asking after George.

BARBARA: Yes, of course you were.

JAMES BEAM: Who would make such a booking? On a day like this, I mean.

BARBARA: An *advance* booking, Professor. - Now, what were they called? - A peculiar name. A group of businessmen. It'll come to me. . . .Ah, yes, the Ancient Order of Blowers. No, that's not quite right . . .*Froth* Blowers, that's it!

[*JAMES BEAM looks staggered by this revelation.*]

You're not a Froth-Blower, Professor Beam?

JAMES BEAM: No, Mrs Foxxe, I am pleased to say.

BARBARA: And on top of all that, George's sister Margaret has decided to pay us a visit from New York. With her advisor and a companion in tow.

JAMES BEAM: You mean, Margaret Foxxe - the Manhattan socialite?

BARBARA: Not exactly academic circles, Professor. No doubt she'll be jet-lagged, too. Well, that settles it, then. I'm going down to the river to prepare everything. Luncheon at five - on the boat.

JAMES BEAM: Isn't that a little late for luncheon, Mrs Foxxe?

BARBARA: The birthday is early and the luncheon is late. It cannot be helped, Professor. Really, it can't.

[BARBARA *turns, moves towards the snug bar, and gives HORACE some curt instructions.*]

JAMES BEAM (*aside*): George isn't the only one who needs his wheels oiled.

BARBARA (*turning*): Did you call me, Professor?

[*JAMES BEAM shakes his head - No, no, no.*]

Oh, I see your glass is empty, Professor. I'll ask Horace to top you up.

[*Speaks to HORACE, then Exits at Stage R. . . .Once again, the wheelchair races across the floor above the ceiling.*]

JAMES BEAM (*listens to wheelchair, aside*): Sounds like he's trying to escape from the studio. Well, there you have it: one day, a man is able-bodied and a bachelor; and the next, he's-.

[*The guests are distracted by the chant of the crowds outside*]:

"DOWN WITH MAYOR FLYNT! DOWN WITH MAYOR FLYNT! UP WITH BOB GREENE!!!

[*The stage lights flicker.*]

S C E N E   T W O

The lounge, seconds later. The lights return to normal. Outside, the chant continues: "DOWN WITH MAYOR FLYNT! WHERE IS MAYOR FLYNT? UP WITH-". Encouraged, ROBERT GREENE motions at HORACE for another beer.

ROBERT GREENE: Not too much froth; there's enough of that at the Mayor's Office.

[*At that, the LAWYER and the MERCHANT BANKER guffaw; the CAMERONS look bewildered, and DR SAXXE-COBURG remains aloof.*]

JEFFERY CAMERON: They're coming, you know. Through the Tunnel. Thousands of them. A cross-Channel link-up with this particular mob.

PHYLLIS CAMERON: How are we going to reach Paris, Jeffrey?

JEFFREY CAMERON: We're not, Phyllis; we're not.

PHYLLIS CAMERON: But this is supposed be our second honeymoon, Jeffrey, and it's a disaster.

JEFFREY CAMERON: It is, Phyllis; it is.

DR SAXXE-COBURG: Look at it this way, Mrs Cameron; at least it will be a memorable second honeymoon.

[*JEFFREY CAMERON looks daringly at DR SAXXE-COBURG.*]

HORACE: I thought you liked a good head, Mr Greene?

ROBERT GREENE: You must be thinking of someone else - (*checks HORACE's name-badge*) - ah, Horace.

HORACE: Yes, that must be it, sir.

[*The pin-striped LAWYER waves a banknote; HORACE ignores the fellow.*]

ROBERT GREENE: You recognise me, then?

HORACE: No, sir.

ROBERT GREENE: You said my name. Just then.

HORACE: Yes, I did, didn't I, sir?

ROBERT GREENE (*struggles to find the right change*): It must have been all that television coverage of the election last month.

HORACE: I don't watch television, sir.

ROBERT GREENE: All right, the newspapers, then.

HORACE: I don't read newspapers, sir.

ROBERT GREENE: Your subconscious, then, has-.

HORACE: -That's not possible, sir.

LAWYER (*to MERCHANT BANKER*): He's not been the same since they put that metal plate in his head.

DR SAXXE-COBURG: Oh really? Of which alloy?

MERCHANT BANKER: Does it matter, Herr Doctor?

DR SAXXE-COBURG: Of course it matters. It matters a very great deal.

PHYLLIS CAMERON: What are they talking about, Jeffrey?

JEFFERY CAMERON: I don't know, Phyllis.

PHYLLIS CAMERON: *Who's* got a metal plate in his head?

JEFFREY CAMERON: I wouldn't like to guess, dear.

HORACE: I remember now, Mr Greene.

ROBERT GREENE: Yes?

HORACE: I heard your name being shouted outside - a moment ago.

ROBERT GREENE: You're mistaken, Horace.

HORACE: I probably am at that, sir.

> [*The LAWYER waves the banknote.*]

I'll be right there, sir.

ROBERT GREENE (*confidentially, to HORACE*): I'm Deputy-Deputy Mayor.

HORACE: Of course you are, sir.

ROBERT GREENE: No, really - I am.

HORACE: Then you're a long way from the Assembly today, Mr Greene.

> [*The LAWYER waves the bank note to no avail.*]

ROBERT GREENE: This is my first afternoon off since my appointment. [*Aside*]: The first, I suspect, of many afternoons off. [*He looks along the red runner, where his gaze happens to fall on JAMES BEAM. They exchange nods as between strangers.*]

HORACE: Sorry, sir?

ROBERT GREENE: Nothing, Horace.

[*HORACE sets up a tray with a fresh drinks; he moves out from behind the bar and crosses to Centre-Stage. At JAMES BEAM's table, he takes the empty glass, then serves the fresh drink.*]

HORACE: How's the jet lag, Professor?

[*At the snug bar, the LAWYER with the banknote looks abandoned.*]

JAMES BEAM: I was thinking of going outside for some fresh air. Do you think that's a good idea, Horace?

[*In the distance, the crowd roars as the riot police encounter resistance at the barricades.*]

HORACE: No, Professor, I do not.

PROFESSOR BEAM: You know, then. You were outside earlier, weren't you? I saw you when you came back. You were sweating. You looked agitated.

HORACE: I'm no agitator, Professor Beam.

JAMES BEAM: I didn't say that you were, Horace. But, ah, what were you doing out there?

HORACE: I was being pursued.

JAMES BEAM: By what?

HORACE: A group of thugs. Demonstrators, if you like. I was on my way back from the Intermezzo Sandwich Bar, when these characters set upon a courier - and knocked him off his bicycle. The courier was delivering a bearer bond. I stepped in and - well, that was that.

JAMES BEAM: You're quite a fellow, aren't you, Horace? How much?

HORACE: The bond? Twenty million Eurodollars. The courier said the merchant bank would send a case of champagne around for my trouble.

JAMES BEAM (*doubtfully*): Well, that's mighty big of them. I'll believe it when I see it. You wouldn't want to leave them short, would you, Horace?

HORACE: That's your subject, isn't it, Professor? Crowd control?

JAMES BEAM: Crowd dynamics. I'm attached to Columbia University. New York and London share many problems in this respect. It's all part of my field study. At what are you grinning, Horace?

HORACE: Nothing, sir.

JAMES BEAM: You hear that?

HORACE: The demonstration?

JAMES BEAM: No, not the demonstration; the wheelchair. [*Lowers voice*]: There's something funny about this wheelchair business; he was perfectly all right just the other day. You know something, Horace, but you won't say.

HORACE: What makes you think that, sir?

JAMES BEAM: He's a prisoner in his own tavern.

HORACE: We're all prisoners today, Professor [*Glances upstage.*] The situation is impossible.

JAMES BEAM: You know something.

HORACE (*reasonably*): I don't know anything about anyone, sir.

JAMES BEAM: Well, know this: I've only known him for three days; but three days is a long time in a place like this. I've become fond if him, which for me isn't easy. We've got to get George out of there. You'll need a pretext. Here, take these cards; they're oily. [*Hands over deck.*] I need a fresh deck. [*HORACE turns.*] You've got the all-clear. She's gone down to the river.

HORACE: I don't think so. She'll be in the kitchen.

JAMES BEAM: She told me-? I get the idea. Okay, when she's gone, we'll make our move.

HORACE: I've got to get back to my post, sir.

JAMES BEAM: Before you go-?

HORACE: Professor?

JAMES BEAM: Who's that fellow in the blue suit? Is he one of these Froth-Blowers?

HORACE (*confidentially*): That's Mr Greene. Deputy-Deputy Mayor.

JAMES BEAM: Well, why doesn't he *do* something?

HORACE: He says it's his afternoon off, Professor.

JAMES BEAM: Would you believe it?

HORACE: Of the Assembly? Yes, sir, I would.

> [*HORACE turns on his heel; retreats to snug bar, and serves the thirsty LAWYER. . .Outside, there are shouts in the distance. Beyond the observation window, the sky starts to change.*]

SCENE THREE

After an interval, the blue-grey sky over Saint Paul's is invaded by the orange-yellow glow of conflict. In the distance, shouts erupt from the barricades followed by a great roar of dissent as the crowd surges against police batons. JAMES BEAM remains at his table; again, he studies the newspaper headlines with unease. . .Outside, a great ice-cream coloured flare explodes without noise, and, after a shower of sparks, is dissipated. The roar of the crowd fades into the background. . .The LAWYER, the MERCHANT BANKER, the CAMERONS, and DR SAXXE-COBURG form a huddle of debate.

PHYLLIS CAMERON: Well, I'm not going to be the one to go outside. Why should I? Or Jeffrey? This is our second honeymoon.

MERCHANT BANKER: So you've said. What's that got to do with it, Mrs Cameron? Why, any one of us could say the same thing. [*Looks doubtful.*]

JEFFREY CAMERON: Phyllis, please. There's no need for anyone to go outside. We're here; we've paid for our rooms. The Eurostar for Paris - well, we'll have to cancel. A high-speed trip to nowhere.

PHYLLIS CAMERON: It might be fun to try, dear. What about you, Herr Doctor?

DR SAXXE-COBURG: What about me, Mrs Cameron? My whole life - as your husband says - has been a high-speed trip to nowhere. I also have paid for my-.

PHYLLIS CAMERON: -You're a bachelor, aren't you?

DR SAXXE-COBURG: I'm a widower.

PHYLLIS CAMERON: Well, that's a kind of bachelor, isn't it? [*To her husband*]: *Isn't* it, Jeffrey?

JEFFREY CAMERON: For God's sake, Phyllis. . .

LAWYER: If anyone should go, it should be . . .? [*Leers along the bar at HORACE and ROBERT GREENE.*]

ROBERT GREENE: I'm running low on cash, Horace. I may have to start a slate.

HORACE: Mr Foxxe does not approve of slates, sir, unless they're on his roof.

ROBERT GREENE: You're trying to be funny, Horace?

HORACE (*fixes his tie*): No, sir, I'm only following standig orders.

ROBERT GREENE: Credit card, then?

HORACE: The merchant terminal's off-line.

ROBERT GREENE: You could use the off-line terminal.

HORACE: I could, but it's jammed.

ROBERT GREENE: I'll try and reach an ATM, then. Do you think that's a good idea?

HORACE: No, sir, I do not. Anyway, the ATMs are probably down. Even if they weren't, you'd never get near one. There's are lot of people out there who are low on cash, too. I could lend you five Eurodollars until-.

ROBERT GREENE: - No, that won't do. I'm going to make a try for it. Besides, I should - really - see how things are out there.

MERCHANT BANKER: It's none of my business, but-.

ROBERT GREENE: You're right about that much.   The people have a right to peaceful assembly.

LAWYER: You call this peaceful . . ?

HORACE: I've bolted the front entrance.

ROBERT GREENE: Back way out of here?

> [*HORACE looks in the direction of the Stage L. portal. ROBERT GREENE crosses the stage to Exit Stage L.*]

PHYLLIS CAMERON: There, you see - he's gone to get help. He's gone to *reason* with them!

HORACE: I don't think so, Mrs Cameron.

JAMES BEAM (*sets paper down*): I don't believe it, either.

MERCHANT BANKER: How do you mean that, Professor? We were - all of us - just discussing who should go outside.

JAMES BEAM: It was something he said . . . The people have a right to-. . .Anyway, why go outside? Soon, everyone will try to get *inside*. Hunger! Thirst! They'll be headed this way - all hundred- thousand of them!

JEFFREY CAMERON (*to his wife*): The Professor studies crowd dynamics.

PHYLLIS CAMERON: Must he?

MERCHANT BANKER: Who, though, studies the Professor?

DR SAXXE-COBURG: An alarmist, nothing more. An American.

LAWYER: If that fellow's with the Mayor's Office, then it's his responsibility to-.

JAMES BEAM: -I don't believe so. A minor bureaucrat?

LAWYER: I *was* going to say: *inform the appropriate authorities*. After all, we all pay our taxes, don't we? [*Looks doubtful. . .The MERCHANT BANKER shies away.*]

JEFFREY CAMERON: Look - it's started!

[*A red-haired, white-faced straggler appears at the portal Stage L. A RED-HEAD protestor detached from the demonstration, she moves to Centre-Stage with a placard marked "SCUM!"*]

MERCHANT BANKER: Is that the face that launched your hundred-thousand, professor?

JAMES BEAM: A pilot fish, that's all. You'll see.

LAWYER (*sneers*): Who's being called scum?

MERCHANT BANKER: Anyone who reads the sign, I suppose.

[*PHYLLIS CAMERON looks askance. . . HORACE sets out a glass of small beer for the RED-HEAD, who moves across stage, then slurps the drink off in one. She leans over the bar, and kisses him on the cheek, and - with a twist of the placard - "THANK YOU!" - Exits at Stage R. HORACE moves after her, and is heard to unbolt the main entrance. He seems to disappear.*]

S C E N E   F O U R

The lights dim slightly. The guests wait in silence. HORACE has not returned. Outside, the sky turns a bright orange, so that the sight of Saint Paul's is obscured by the glare. London is burning, or so it seems. . . the observation window frames the spectacle to extraordinary effect. JAMES BEAM reads his paper. The guests by the snug bar are almost hypnotised by the pyrotechnics, then - after a great yellow flash in the sky - the orange hue retreats. Once more, the blue-grey sky above St Paul's begins to re-assert itself.

PHYLLIS CAMERON: Isn't anyone going to check on Horace? Jeffrey?

JEFFREY CAMERON: He's probably gone after that Mr Greene. What do you say, Professor?

JAMES BEAM: Not a chance. The red-head, maybe.

LAWYER (*to the group*): I think we'd better have that little meeting now.

JAMES BEAM (*aside*): And so Horace is abandoned.

[*The group moves across to Stage L., and - one by one - climb into the cubicle.*]

MERCHANT BANKER: Joining us, Professor?

JAMES BEAM: Democracy in action? Not just now, thank you.

LAWYER: Your democratic instincts intact, Professor?

JAMES BEAM: I'd get more sense out of a donkey. [*In the distance, BOOs and BAYs.*]

[*The group discusses 'the issues' among themselves.*]

[*HORACE reappears at Stage R.: he crosses to Centre-Stage, and sets the fresh deck of cards on JAMES BEAM's table*].

The most attractive demonstrator I've seen in a while. Don't you think so, Horace? A fine-looking rioter-. If she's representative, I might even join the fray myself. There's life in the old goat yet, Horace. [*Puffs cigar.*]

HORACE (*breathless*): - In my opinion, Professor Beam . . .we'll all be-. . .better off when we . . .get down to the river.

JAMES BEAM: In *your* opinion? Didn't you know that in your opinion that's supposed to be a surprise? A pleasant surprise, presumably.

HORACE (*off-balance*): Yes, sir. Sorry, sir. I'd be grateful, Professor, if you would pretend to look surprised when Mr Foxxe makes the announcement.

[*A merry-sounding wheelchair shifts back- and-forth across the ceiling above the lounge; a light sprinkling of dust drops onto the crimson carpet below.*]

JAMES BEAM (*glances at the ceiling*): I'll try, Horace, I'll surely try. . .Sounds like old George is raring to get out of there. Been locked up too long. Cabin fever, is my guess.

HORACE: It'll do Mr Foxxe good to get some fresh air for a change.

JAMES BEAM: Fresh air? You mean there's fresh air out there? Anyone following you, Horace?

HORACE (*at mid-stage*): No, sir, I managed to-. [*Returns to snug bar*]: I mean, no sir, of course not. . .[*Turns, opens the dumb waiter - sees that it is loaded - closes it again, and sends the contraption rattling down the shaft into the kitchen, where there is a CRASH! of crockery and cutlery. From below, there is a muffled shout of protest.*]

BARBARA (*off-stage*): HORACE! BE *CAREFUL* - WON'T YOU? - YOU SILLY MAN! YOU'LL KILL SOMEONE ONE OF THESE DAYS! Why don't you-? [*The rest is lost as HORACE slams the shutter.*]

HORACE: Now, Professor, may I refresh your drink?

JAMES BEAM: Sure. [*Looks at the group Stage L.*] It's a time for some big decisions, all right.

HORACE: The Bank of England. I hear it's under siege, Professor.

[*Outside the observation window, a great, silent, orange plume of gas and flame rises: it looks like a vision of Hell, then the apparition fades, and the dome of St Paul's reemerges from the conflagration.*]

JAMES BEAM: Who told you that? The red-head?

[*HORACE checks the time, but finds that his wristwatch has disappeared. Feels at his naked wrist; then, accepting that his watch is lost, prepares the drink.*]

JAMES BEAM: Didn't take your watch, did she?

HORACE: No, sir. I'm always losing it. [*Moves to Centre-Stage.*] It'll turn up.

BARBARA (*appears Stage R.*): Horace? Horace! What was that about losing it? Your temper, you must mean?

HORACE (*alert*): Mrs Foxxe?

BARBARA: Oh, please, Horace, there's no need to over-react.

[*JAMES BEAM watches this performance while he re-lights his cigar.*]

HORACE (*moves*): Yes, Mrs Foxxe. [*Turns, stops.*]

BARBARA: Is this yours, Horace? [*Shows a closed fist.*]

HORACE: I don't know. I can't see-.

[*BARBARA unclasps her fist to reveal the lost wristwatch.*]

Thank you, Mrs Foxxe. I've been looking for that everywhere.

[HORACE *steps forward, and takes the watch . . . He puts the timepiece on, and smiles upstage.*]

BARBARA: Clearly not *everywhere*, Horace.

HORACE (*loses smile*): Mrs Foxxe . . ?

BARBARA: Not, say, in the dumb waiter, which for some reason you persistently abuse.

HORACE: It must have . . .fallen down the shaft and into the kitchen. . .

BARBARA (*arms folded*): I've told you before, Horace, not to treat the dumb waiter so shoddily. . .

[*JAMES BEAM looks on with incredulity.*]

HORACE: Yes, Mrs Foxxe.

BARBARA (*unfolds arms*): Now, there's work to do. [*Looks around.*] Where is everyone?

JAMES BEAM: They're in a meeting. [*Points a thumb over his shoulder.*]

BARBARA: All right, everyone, if you'd please pay attention. . . You're all invited for luncheon on the riverboat

[*JAMES BEAM pretends to look as surprised as the group in the cubicle. HORACE grins.*]

Five o'clock for six. We'll try and lay on a taxi - if that's at all possible.

[*She turns and marches along the crimson runner to Exit Stage R. The group in the cubicle finds a new dimension to their debate.*]

BARBARA (*off-stage*): Oh, Horace? A quick word, if you please.

[HORACE *marches along the runner, and disappears through the archway void Stage R.*]

Horace, who was that girl I saw you with?

HORACE (*off-stage*): Which girl, Mrs Foxxe?

JAMES BEAM (*aside*): That's redheads for you: trouble. Red-heads with a placard: more trouble. Red-heads as pretty as that?: dive for cover, Horace.

PHYLLIS CAMERON: You have something you want to add, Professor?

JAMES BEAM: Not at this time, Mrs Cameron.

MERCHANT BANKER: Well, that's it, then. It looks like we're unable to reach a decision.

LAWYER: I suggest we drop hands.

PHYLLIS CAMERON (*rationally*): I think Barbara Foxxe is right: we should forget about the whole thing, and go down to the river for lunch. Either that or we could make a try for the Eurostar at St. Pancras - and get out of this city all together. What do you think, Jeffrey?

JEFFREY CAMERON: I don't know what to think.

PHYLLIS CAMERON: Herr Doctor?

DOCTOR SAXXE-COBURG: As an idea, I think it is interesting. As a plan of action, either way, it is the craziest thing I've heard in years. However, I am game if you all are. The train or the river. You all decide.

[*JAMES BEAM puffs on his cigar and chuckles to himself.*]

JEFFREY CAMERON: What do you think, Professor Beam?

JAMES BEAM: We don't have much choice. Any way you look it, I think we've just been given our marching orders.

DR SAXXE-COBURG: In that case, I shall demand a refund!

[*THE LAWYER and the MERCHANT BANKER yelp and guffaw.*]

S C E N E   F I V E

Outside the lounge window, a "fireworks" display erupts, then subsides, and the dome of St Paul's reasserts itself against a dark-grey skyline. The lighting in the lounge is subdued; the warm yellow lights of the snug bar stand out, but there is no sign of HORACE. The group remains inside the cubicle; JAMES BEAM tries to read his newspaper. Footsteps are heard climbing the stairwell to the portal at Stage L. Seconds later, a man in an expensive, but disheveled, business suit appears: CARLTON GREY, his face covered with sweat, steps onto the crimson carpet, which seems to carry him towards JAMES BEAM's table.

JAMES BEAM (*disconcerted*): You're with the demonstration?

CARLTON GREY (*labours for breath*): I am not, sir. I did pass *through* it, though.

JAMES BEAM: You'd better sit down. The bartenter'll be back soon.

CARLTON GREY (*sits at table*): Do I look like I need a drink?

JAMES BEAM: If I may say so - Yes.

CARLTON GREY: Ah, interesting carpet. I don't think I've seen anything quite like it

JAMES BEAM: The proprietor told me it was brought down the Khyber Pass on a donkey. The donkey fell down a gorge, but the carpet survived. Back in the 1990s, there was a fire here. Five or maybe six people were killed - a tour guide and his group. That's the story, anyway. Somehow, once again, the carpet survived.

CARLTON GREY: I've heard that story.

JAMES BEAM: You have? Why didn't you stop me?

CARLTON GREY: You seemed to enjoy telling it.

JAMES BEAM: You're a tourist, then?

CARLTON GREY: Do I look like a tourist?

JAMES BEAM: Not exactly.

CARLTON GREY: I was looking for George Foxxe, Mr-.

JAMES BEAM: James Beam - Professor - attached to Columbia University.

CARLTON GREY: I've crossed the Atlantic, then, to meet a fellow New Yorker? My name is Carlton Grey - advisor to Margaret Foxxe.

JAMES BEAM: Would that be Mrs Margaret Foxxe, of Manhattan - the socialite?

CARLTON GREY: It would, Professor, though I'm not sure she'd entirely appreciate the appellation. I was looking for her brother George. I tried to get through on the mobile, but - (*shows a khaki mobile*) - it's immobilised.

JAMES BEAM: It was a miracle you got through yourself. As for George - (*listens for the wheelchair*) - he and I usually have a game of cards at this hour, but - well, Mrs Foxxe says he's resting.

CARLTON GREY: Mrs Foxxe? That cannot be right. I'm the advance party for Mrs Foxxe and her travelling companion, Miss Wichell. We're staying at The Savoy.

JAMES BEAM: Where else? But I don't mean that Mrs Foxxe. I meant his wife, Mrs Foxxe. . .

MR GREY: You probably don't realise, Professor Beam: George isn't married. Or rather he was, but his wife - Eva Foxxe - died in that same tragedy you've already mentioned.

[*CARLTON GREY realises he has an audience in the form of the cubicle group; he becomes uncomfortable.*]

JAMES BEAM: Advance party? Are things really that bad?

CARLTON GREY: I should say they are: the ladies decided that I should go on ahead to-.

JAMES BEAM: - Well, I suppose they would. Why risk your own neck when you can risk someone else's? [Aside]: The way of plutocrats everywhere.

CARLTON GREY: I'm a vet.

PHYLLIS CAMERON (*to the group*): He's interested in animals!

CARLTON GREY (*aside*): Not those kind of animals, lady, and not that kind of vet. Special forces. The Gulf. North Korea.

PHYLLIS CAMERON: Well, whatever kind, you're a real-life hero, Mr Grey; I recognised you as soon as you stepped-in that door.

CARLTON GREY: Why, thank you.

JEFFREY CAMERON: We - ah, that is, the group - were wondering, Mr Grey, if you have any advice concerning the current situation.

CARLTON GREY: Advice?

JEFFREY CAMEROIN: Well, yes, about what might be our best course of action. You know, a plan of attack - as it were.

CARLTON GREY (*considers, then decides*): I'm retired. I'm an investor in strategic futures now.

PHYLLIS CAMERON: Oh.

JAMES BEAM: Well, it looks like you've come to the right city, Mr Grey.

CARLTON GREY (*to the group*): Besides, I have no idea what's going on here. We've only just arrived in your fine country.

[*The wheelchair creak-creak-creaks across the floor above. CARLTON GREY reluctantly looks at the ceiling. Outside, a great, blinding-white flare shoots across the sky, so that CARLTON GREY jerks his arm across his face - involuntarily - to protect his eyes. The flare dies down, and is extinguished.*]

CARLTON GREY (*stands*): I'd better report back to The Savoy. Situation Report. I'll call back again later. Nice meeting you folks. Good luck with your meeting. [*Waves.*] You, too, Professor Beam.

[*PHYLLIS CAMERON returns the wave from the cubicle.*]

JAMES BEAM: Be sure you're not recognised.

CARLTON GREY: Recognised? By who-?

JAMES BEAM: The people at the barricades. You've got through once already. In that suit, they'll see you coming a mile away.

CARLTON GREY: This suit cost me five-thousand dollars. What's wrong with it?

JAMES BEAM: That's what's wrong with it. It makes you a target - an expensive one at that.

CARLTON GREY: Yes, I see what you mean. Thanks for the advice, Professor. Back way out of here?

JAMES BEAM: Over there.

[*CARLTON GREY departs Stage L. portal.*]

SCENE SIX

JAMES BEAM takes a deep breath. Outside, the rioters are silent. and there is an interlude of real peace at The Arms. The cubicle group engages in casual banter.

JAMES BEAM (*to the stairwell void*): Horace! Are you there?

HORACE (off-stage): No, Professor, I'm - [*his voice is lost.*]

> [*After an interval, Enter Stage R. ROBERT GREENE followed by HORACE. The men take up their former positions either side of the snug bar.*]

ROBERT GREENE: What's the occasion, Horace?

HORACE: Mr Foxxe's birthday. Everyone's invited, Mr Greene. Mrs Foxxe's instructions.

> [*JAMES BEAM rises from the table and approaches the snug bar.*]

JAMES BEAM: How's everything outside?

ROBERT GREENE: Everything is under control, sir; there's no need for alarm.

JAMES BEAM: I'm not alarmed. Same again, Horace. . . I was just asking, that's all. You're with the Mayor's Office, I presume?

> [*HORACE's eyes shift as he pours the beer.*]

ROBERT GREENE: Then I should apologise for this situation on behalf of the Mayor's Office. As you are a tourist in our great city, let me assure you - London is not usually so unsettled.

JAMES BEAM: I'm not a tourist. A risky strategy going out there.

ROBERT GREENE: I tried to reach an ATM. Impossible. After that, I went to the Intermezzo Sandwich Bar. It was closed. It was more than closed. . . I'll pay you back those Eurodollars first thing tomorrow, Horace. [*Pays for his drink.*]

HORACE (*to GREENE*): Professor Beam is attached the Columbia University.

ROBERT GREENE: That's in New York, isn't it?

JAMES BEAM: Ever been to New York, Mr Greene?

ROBERT GREENE: Only once; for a few days last year.

JAMES BEAM: Is that so?

ROBERT GREENE: Yes, I was part of a London delegation to meet with your Mayor Gambini.

HORACE: Professor Beam studies . . .crowd dynamics.

JAMES BEAM: Academic interest.

ROBERT GREENE: Academic? Well, Professor, I'm sure you'll find plenty to interest you in London.

JAMES BEAM: I'll drink to that. [*The two men raise their glasses, and swallow.*]

JAMES BEAM (*to HORACE*): You were saying about George? You have instructions?

HORACE: I do. And you have your fresh deck of cards, Professor. [*Winks.*] Mr Foxxe sent them down with the compliments of the house.

JAMES BEAM: You've seen him, then?

HORACE: I only saw his hand, sir.

JAMES BEAM: His hand? How do you know it was his hand? Explain, if you would.

HORACE: Explain? Well, sir. . .I was speaking with him through the door, sir, and then the door opened - only slightly, mind you - and out came this hand holding a deck of cards. Spooky, it was, sir. The voice told me to take the deck of cards, and then the hand disappeared, and the door closed. The voice told me to give the cards to you, Professor Beam, and only you. Oh, and the voice said the deck may be a card short, and that you'd better check. [*Winks, again.*]

ROBERT GREENE: The voice, Horace? I take it you mean Mr Foxxe's voice?

HORACE: Yes, Mr Greene, that's what I meant.

JAMES BEAM: Are you sure, Horace, it wasn't a woman's hand?

HORACE (*sidles up to dumb waiter*): Oh no, sir: You don't catch me on that one . . .It was Mr Foxxe's hand, for sure.

ROBERT GREENE: Did the voice say anything else?

HORACE: You mean, sir, did Mr Foxxe say anything else?

ROBERT GREENE: Yes, that's what I meant. Well, did he?

HORACE: Like what, Mr Greene?

ROBERT GREENE (*shrugs*): Well, I don't know - I wasn't there, was I?

[*HORACE falters.*]

JAMES BEAM: Did the voi-? [*Corrects himself*]: Did George say why he was lying so low these days? [*The two men at the snug look up at the ceiling.*] Well, did he . . .?

HORACE: Yes, sir, he did, sir. Something about - the Conglomerate.

JAMES BEAM: The Conglomerate?

HORACE: I've been with him for twenty-five years. I've never seen him like this . . .He seems - (*looks between the two men, then at the portal Stage R.*) - to be turning in on himself.

JAMES BEAM: That'll do, Horace. You never know who might be listening.

ROBERT GREENE: Who, for instance?

HORACE: The Conglomerate, sir.

ROBERT GREENE: The Conglomerate. . ? [*Aside*]: That's corporate affairs, perhaps, not my section. [*To HORACE*]: What are you talking about? Did the voice tell you this?

HORACE: Yes, sir. You're - not with the Conglomerate, are you, Mr Greene?

ROBERT GREENE: No, of course not! I've already told you! I'm-.

HORACE: - Just enquiring, sir.

HORACE (*turns*): And you, Professor? Are you with the Conglomerate, sir?

[*JAMES BEAM has already turned away. At the Centre-Stage table, he sits to inspect the fresh deck of cards. A card seems to be missing; in its place, a note, which he pulls out and reads. His eyebrows jump as he looks upstage.*]

ROBERT GREENE: You haven't you got a full deck, Professor Beam?

JAMES BEAM: Horace, we've got to get him out of there. You go on ahead, to the riverboat. She'll be expecting you. Don't say anything about George. If you're asked, say he's having soup in the studio. I'll take care of the wheelchair. [*To the cubicle group*]: It's time we all got down to where the river bends.

PHYLLIS CAMERON: We're not going, Professor. We've decided to stay here.

JEFFREY CAMERON: We have?

JAMES BEAM: Then lock yourselves in your rooms.

> [*The action freezes: everyone on stage becomes immobilised. Outside the window, great columns of smoke and gas are taking shape, leaping into the late-afternoon sky above the dome of St Paul's - like grey flames, or the memory of flames.*
>
> *At the Stage L. portal, a man in a red blazer appears. This is MR SHINE, the tour guide, who spots the crimson carpet, and is delighted. He steps onto the end of the carpet, and at the same time he is followed by a group of tourists dressed in the winter fashion of the 1990s. The entire group, led by MR SHINE, progresses - slowly, slowly - along the crimson carpet from Stage L. to Centre-Stage. Everyone already on stage is oblivious of this group. Outside the window, the grey plumes are at full burn above St Paul's . . .*]

MR SHINE (*moving, slowly*): It was here, at The Arms, that the opponents of Robert Walpole gathered to plot against the then Prime Minister . . .

MR STOKER (*with an American accent*): Is this guy Walpole still around, Mr Shine?

MR SHINE (*astonished, but politely*): Oh, no, Mr Stoker - that was a long, long time ago. But I'll grant you this - Mr Walpole was around for a long, long time, too. [*Smiles.*]

MISS ASHE (*a tourist at rear of group, sniffs*): Mr Shine, I can smell something burning. . .

MR SHINE (*jauntily, over his should*): That, Miss Ashe, is an aroma from the kitchen. The Arms, you know, is famous for its roast beef.

MISS ASHE: Smells more like . . .pork.

> [*MISS ASHE sniffs again, and frowns, dissatisfied . . .The group has now reached the archway at Stage R. The group huddles, almost comically, around MR SHINE as though for protection. The group is unaware of the men at the snug bar, except for MR STOKER, who, with his hands in his tweed overcoat, leers suspiciously at HORACE. The group, one by one, disappears into the archway void.*]

MISS ASHE (*off-stage*): Mr Shine, I could feel a presence in there.

MR SHINE (*off-stage, confidentially*): Well, I for one, Miss Ashe, do not believe in ghosts. Do yoooou?

MISS ASHE (*off-stage, affronted*): I wouldn't like to say.

MR SHINE (*off-stage*): Come along now, Mr Stoker, it's time to take a walk along the river.

> [*A baffled MR STOKER looks upstage for an explanation, turns, and disappears through the archway void . . .. Outside, the great grey plumes subside, and the dome of St Paul's emerges, illuminated sharply against the cityscape.*]

JAMES BEAM (*unfreezing*): You ever have that feeling you're not alone?

> [*HORACE grins with satisfaction, and takes to polishing a beerglass, which sparkles under the light of the snug bar.*]

ROBERT GREENE: You know, gentlemen, I have heard it said that this place is haunted.

JAMES BEAM: Who told you that?

ROBERT GREENE: You know, I don't recall.

JAMES BEAM: Well, is it true, Horace? Is this place-?

[*Both men look to HORACE for an answer. The group exits the cubicle and crosses the stage to approach the snug bar.*]

HORACE: I wouldn't like to say. It's beyond my understanding, that kind of thing. Occasionally, I've seen an old customer pass this way.

ROBERT GREENE: That's not quite the same thing, Horace, is it?

HORACE (*polishing*): Well, that depends on the customer   -   wouldn't you agree?

[*Lights suddenly to dark. HORACE drops the glass he has been polishing - it crashes to the floor! . . .At this, a spotlight appears at Stage-Centre. BAKUNIN, The WILD MAN in the long, grey trenchcoat appears under the spotlight, and peers - bug-eyed - upstage. He takes out his pocket watch.*]

BAKUNIN: I have an appointment on the water. [*Looks at watch.*] I'll see you all down by the river.

[*Looks, wild-eyed, Stage R. and, running, - with the spotlight tracking him along the crimson carpet - he hurls himself through the archway void.*

Spotlight lingers, shrinks to a spot, then dark.

CURTAINS.]

ACT II

The canopied deck of a substantial riverboat forms the set. The notional aspect, then, is a tableau aft of the pilothouse - with a view over the stern onto the Thames: the City of London by night, and - in the distance, displaced towards Stage L. - the illuminated dome of Saint Paul's, which rises above the downstage Embankment.

An off-stage gangway stretches from the Embankment to reach the riverboat at Stage L. A long dining table (as at The Arms, ACT I) is positioned at Stage-Centre. At downstage from this, tied to white-painted rails, a red-and-white lifebelt shows stencil lettering: MIKHAIL B. MV. . .

At Stage R., a stairwell opens onto a void (as at The Arms), which descends into an off-stage galley. An occasional puff of water vapour billows from the galley. At corner Stage R., a service area contains a cocktail bar, desklamp, a telephone extension, and control panel.

SCENE ONE

Curtains. Lights. A spectacular view of the riverboat deck. The lights of the Thames blink and shimmer. In the distance, the dome of Saint Paul's is bathed in a warm, orange glow, with wisps of smoke billowing up into the night sky. On the deck, the lighting is subdued, and is provided by several chinese lanterns suspended from the canopy. The dining table is set with linen, silver service, and wineglasses. Candles, as yet unlit.

In the distance, there is a muffled roar from the mob, and a great plume of white of smoke goes up over the Embankment. A distinct cheer is followed by a banshee-like wail, and a police-whistle, which sets a dog off barking - and then silence, except for the lap-lap-lap of the river against the hull of the boat. A fuse starts burning, which HORACE - appearing at Stage R. - snuffs out with his bare fingers.

HORACE wears a formal dark-tie outfit. His hair has been combed-down severely to one side of his head. The sky glows, so that HORACE - as he moves along the length of the dining table - is almost in silhouette. At mid-table, he spots a fork, which he seems to set askew - deliberately. He stiffens.

BARBARA *(off-stage)*: Horace? Are you there, Horace? [*She appears Stage R. in a sapphire-blue cocktail dress*]: I was in the galley . . .I thought I heard you calling. Look, I'm ruining this dress. [*Saunters onto the deck*]: Everything all right at The Arms? Where are the guests? Where for, that matter, is the rest of the staff? [*Under a lantern, she looks at her tiny wristwatch. She taps at it, without success.*]

[*HORACE does not know which question to answer first.*]

Well, Horace . .?

HORACE: Everything is secure, Mrs Foxxe. The guests are on their way. Mr and Mrs Cameron have decided to stay in their room. [*Remains Centre-Stage.*]

BARBARA: It's their second honeymoon. I suppose they'll watch television or play cards - or something.

HORACE (*smirks*): Yes, Mrs Foxxe.

BARBARA: Is that your full report?

HORACE: Yes, Mrs Foxxe. No, Mrs Foxxe: the staff. The staff have taken the night off.

BARBARA: Oh, they have, have they? And whose bright idea was that?

HORACE: Their own.

BARBARA: I see. And what about you, Horace? Why haven't you taken the night off?

HORACE: I don't have nights off, Mrs Foxxe.

BARBARA: Why ever not? You're trying to make an exception? - of yourself?

HORACE: I hadn't thought of it that way - but, no. George always says the night you take off is the night something will happen.

BARBARA (*considers*): Do you think that's true?

HORACE: I wouldn't know, Mrs Foxxe. I've never had a night off.

BARBARA (*smirks*): Well, we'll just have to make do, won't we - you and I. . ? [*Moves a step closer; notices downstage view*]: What a wonderful evening, Horace! You see, how time stands still on the river? Why, on a night like this, I feel I could live forever!

HORACE: Yes, Mrs Foxxe.

BARBARA (*on the subject*): And darling George?

HORACE: Darling George is just fine, Mrs Foxxe.

BARBARA: What did you say?

HORACE: Ah, Mr Foxxe is having soup in his studio.

BARBARA: I see. And did he say anything to you, Horace?

HORACE: He wasn't entirely coherent; he didn't say anything as such.

BARBARA: As such? What does that mean?

HORACE: He appears to be under medication of some kind. He used hand signals.

BARBARA: And what did these hand signals say?

HORACE: I don't know, Mrs Foxxe; the hand signals were incoherent, too.

[*A great white flare scars the night sky, and frizzles out in the river.*]

BARBARA (*relieved*): Oh look, Horace! What a wonderful firework display! [*Peers*]: They *are* fireworks, aren't they?

HORACE: Of a kind, Mrs Foxxe.

[*She looks at him - in an incomprehensible way - from under a chinese lantern.*]

Flares, I would say. [*He is uneasy under her eyes.*]

BARBARA: Anything else to report? Any sign of George's sister? Any calls?

HORACE: The networks, it seems, are being subjected to some kind of electronic fog. There's no way she could get a message through - unless by a runner.

BARBARA: A runner?

HORACE: And there's no sign of the Frothblowers, either, Mrs Foxxe.

BARBARA (*moves Centre-Stage*): You know, I'd completely forgotten about the Blowers.

HORACE: - Frothblowers.

BARBARA (*chuckles*): Yes, of course. . .They've probably cancelled, too. But just in case, once things settle here, I'll go back up to The Arms and make sure. Agreed?

HORACE (*keen*): Agreed, Mrs Foxxe.

BARBARA: We make quite a team, don't we? Who needs the rest of the staff? You know, Horace, one day soon, when this is all over-. . .

HORACE: When what's all over, Mrs Foxxe?

[*She notices the fork askew on the table.*]

BARBARA: I was going to say-. Oh, look, Horace, you silly man. Why don't you watch how you set the table! That fork there! [*Glares at him*]: What will George's sister think of us?

HORACE: But-?

BARBARA: - She'll be here, all right. Nothing on this Earth would stop her. They're late, that's all. It's only a question of how late? A trip to Europe indeed - it's nothing but a bit of real estate to her; Europe, I mean. Don't repeat that, Horace - ever.

HORACE (*pulls out pocketwatch on a chain*): Under the circumstances, Mrs Foxxe, don't you think we should allow the guests a little leeway? [*Note: The pocket watch is the same as BAKUNIN's.*]

BARBARA: Circumstances? George's sister is probably waiting for her nail varnish to dry, that's all. As for leeway, as far as I'm concerned, they can have all the leeway they want. [*Eyes the gold watch*]: Where did you get that, Horace?

HORACE (*about to put away the watch*): My great, great grandfather's. He was a Russian.

BARBARA (*grabbing*): Here, let me see that-. [*She tug-tugs, so that HORACE's waistcoat is pulled away from his chest. At Centre-Stage, they struggle at either end of the chain.*] Now, stay still, Horace! [*Studies the back of the watch, reading*]: Eighteen Forty-Eight. . ![*Frowns*]: It must be very valuable.

HORACE: I don't know about that.

BARBARA: Well, you should find out. Are you sure it doesn't belong to George . . ? [*Releases the chain.*]

HORACE (*at the end of an impromptu pendulum*): No, ma'am, it belonged - (*catches the swinging watch*) - to my great, great grandfather.

BARBARA: Did you say he was a Russian? But your name is Baker - Horace Baker - that's not Russian!

HORACE (*demurely*): The family name was changed.

BARBARA: From what--?

HORACE: -Baku-. Bakunin!

BARBARA (*tries again, smiling*): Here - give me!

HORACE: Ha! Ha! Ha-ha! [*Recovers chain; conceals the timepiece.*]

BARBARA (*relaxes*): You know, I've never heard you laugh before. That was a laugh, wasn't it?

[*After a pause . . .a tidal surge moves up-river, so that HORACE and BARBARA shift on their feet. A fork falls from the table to the deck.*]

BARBARA: What was that, Horace?

HORACE: That was the tide. [*Chances*]: - from an old barge.

BARBARA (*excited*): Why yes - I could feel the whole boat move beneath me!

[*Breathless*]: Anyway, everything is ready. I can't see what else we can do, except wait . . . [*Recovers, waltzes along the length of the table to Stage C; stoops to pick up the fork, sets it straight.*] Everything must be perfect. [*She notices another fork askew; she glances at HORACE for an explanation.*]

HORACE: It was the surge.

BARBARA: Horace, you-. [*She bites her lip.*] I think - I think - we're going to have to review your employment with the company, Horace.

HORACE: The company? George - Mr Foxxe - employs me.

BARBARA (*takes a step downstage, into the shadows*): That may be so now, but I'm not talking about now, I'm talking about eventualities. These old family firms won't last. They've had their day. No one has their own children any more. They have no leverage, because they have no shareholders - no investors, Horace.

HORACE: Shareholders, Mrs Foxxe?

BARBARA (*her face deep in shadow*): Shareholders, Horace. That's people with an equity stake in the firm.

HORACE (*remotely*): But you're . . . his wife?

BARBARA: I know I'm his wife. This last month now.

HORACE: If I might say .. ?

BARBARA: Of course you may say. Freely. Say anything that comes into your head, Horace. From now on - you and I-? Well, we have a special relationship. Say the first thing that comes into your head. Why not? Everyone else does.

[*BARBARA is so far into the downstage shadows, she is barely visible - except for her cocktail dress. HORACE, restless, moves downstage, wanders around the Stage L.-end of the dining table, and takes up a position by the lifebelt marked MIKHAIL B., MV. He stares into the dark waters of the river.*]

Well .. ?

HORACE: I'll try. . .Ah, bedknobs. Jaberwocky. The Fleet runs deep. Into. Old Father Thames. Knickerbocker Glory. Anarchy and Amberjacks. Ah, custard tarts with nutmeg. Down with Mayor Flynt. Up with Bob Greene . . .I'll be right there, Mr Shine.

BARBARA: -Horace! Horace! -That's not what I meant. I want you to open up your mind.

HORACE: I am opening up my mind, Mrs Foxxe, and that's what came out. There's much more.

BARBARA: I believe you. A river of ambrosia, I'm sure-. [*She bites her lip.*] Let me assist you. Try this: after all these years working for George, and what have you got?

HORACE: I've drawn a blank.

BARBARA: Indeed you have. Nothing!

HORACE: I have my ancestor's watch.

BARBARA: Try this, then: you have nothing, but don't your owe anyone anything - except yourself.

HORACE: This is becoming complicated, Mrs Foxxe.

BARBARA: You owe him nothing.

HORACE (*embarrassed*): I owe him my - my, er, loyalty.

[*In the far, far distance, there are howls of disapproval.*]

BARBARA: How old-fashioned you are, really. What a bore you are, after all. I must express profound disappointment.

HORACE (*tries to impress*): I've done questionable things in my time, Mrs Foxxe. Things - only blurred memories, really - which don't bear talking about.

BARBARA (*interested*): You have?

HORACE: When I said about owing him my-. I meant it just that way. So - it's not for sale. Like everything else around here.

BARBARA: Why, you-! [*She gathers her dress at one side.*] How tedious! I was expecting more imagination from you, Horace.

HORACE: Imagination? [*As though waking up*]: Then, try this: You. You're not Mrs Foxxe. That Mrs Foxxe is dead. You're just plain Barbara. You're with the Conglomerate, aren't you? You're their - creature.

BARBARA: If you're going to start talking like that, Horace, you'd better find yourself a lawyer. A very good lawyer.

HORACE: George was right all along: they're moving in. That's why you've been keeping him upstairs-. Today and tonight, though, things have not gone your way. You never counted on all of this-. Or the early birthday.

BARBARA (*jauntily, steps upstage into the lantern-light*): I don't know what you're talking about, Horace. I do believe you've been drinking.

HORACE: Not yet, I haven't.

BARBARA: And we all know what happens to employees who've been drinking on duty, don't we? Instant dismissal! Kaput! [*She claps her hands together as she moves to Center Stage, and turns her back upstage.*] So, we've had our little talk together, Horace, and I'm pleased to say you've passed - the test!

HORACE: Test? What test?

BARBARA: Why, the loyalty test, of course! [*Turns her back on him, faces upstage*]: Oh, what a wonderful evening! And to think my darling husband is in such safe hands!

[*HORACE, bewildered, gawps at her, then casts his eyes at the deck. He moves along the downstage-rails - away from the lifebelt - to Stage L. They are, in effect, circling one another.*]

From now on, you and I are going to be good friends! Understand, Horace?

HORACE: Yes, Mrs Fooxe - if you say so.

BARBARA: And you'll call me Barbara. Isn't that right, Horace?

HORACE (*moves slowly along the rails*): Yes, Mrs Foxxe. If you say so.

BARBARA: Yes, what . . ?

HORACE (*halts*): Yes . . .Barbara. [*Looks as though he might throw himself overboard.*]

BARBARA (*halts*): Now, where were we? I'd better be getting back to the galley. I wouldn't want to burn anything. You see what happens when the cowardly staff runs away? - I'm left to do everything! Everything, Horace. So, don't let me down this evening, will you? You won't run away like the others, will you?

HORACE: No, ah . . .Barbara

BARBARA: That's much better. I like the way you say my name, Horace. It's not as easy a name to say as people suppose. [*Looks up at the canopy*]: Now, first-. It would be useful-. I mean, are you acquainted with George's sister? What does she - ahm - want here exactly?

HORACE (*listless*): Want? I don't think Margaret Foxxe wants for anything. I understand London is the first stop of a European tour -.

[*BARBARA checks her tiny wristwatch, and is surprised.*]

- with her companion, a Miss Wichell-. Also, Mr Grey, her advisor.

BARBARA: Who? - Oh look, Horace! It's moving again. You know what that means, don't you?

HORACE: What does it mean?

BARBARA: It means . . . that our guests are not late, and it means our little conversation took no time at all. In fact, it - never took place.

HORACE: I should not, then, call you-?

BARBARA: Not in front of the others. They might get ideas.

[*A dreadful groan sounds from belowdecks: ARGGW-WWWWANNNN!!!!*]

HORACE! HORACE! What's *that*? [*Seized by panic, her eyes bulge.*] What was that? [*She listens, but it is done.*]

HORACE (*calmly*): Probably the bilges.

BARBARA: Oh, oh, ohhhh. You and your bilges, Horace! [*Laughs, sharply.*] For a moment, I thought-. Oh, never mind what I thought. But you know what they say about The Arms, don't

you? [*HORACE ignores the question.*] I thought it was - you
know - down *here*, too. You must think I'm foolish - but,
well, -.

[*BARBARA is shaking inside her sapphire-blue cocktail
dress; HORACE offers her no reassurance.*]

You'd better call The Arms, Horace. Find out if they're on
their way.

HORACE (*hesitates*): Yes, Mrs Fo-. [*Moves to Stage R., takes a
position at the service area control panel. Checks the
telephone extension. Grabs a mobile unit; this, too, is dead.*]

BARBARA (*remains Centre-Stage*): Well . . ?

HORACE (*looks at Embankment, Stage L*): It's dead. They're all
dead!

BARBARA: They're probably trying to hail a taxi.

[*In the distance, the rioters find their voice again, and a
great roar goes up into the night as a barricade falls. . .
BARBARA struts, and looks downstage, perturbed.*]

HORACE: A taxi? I don't think so. On a night like this, not even
the Mayor himself could hail a taxi.

[*Returns the telephone to its receiver with a* clonk.]

BARBARA: I'm sure they'll find a way through. [*Nearby, there is a
SPLASH! HORACE moves downstage where he looks over
the rails and into the river.*]

[*BARBARA casts her eyes at the canopy. HORACE climbs
over the rails - as far as he can go - and reaches into the
water.*]

BARBARA (*moves downstage*): What are you looking at, Horace?
What, Horace, are you looking at?

HORACE (*head out of sight*): The river. [*He starts to slide, but grabs with one hand at the lifebelt.*]

BARBARA (*stands erect*): Horace! Horace!

[*HORACE, with a lunge, vaults over the rails, and lands on the deck - a placard clutched in one hand.*]

[*Breathless*]: I said-?

HORACE (*straightens his hair*): - Someone's trying to get a message to us.

BARBARA: Who? What message? [*Peeved*]: That girl I saw you with, no doubt. Anything - important?

[*She moves downstage and confronts him. HORACE hides the placard behind his back.*]

BARBARA (*closer again*): What does that sign say? You're trying to frighten me, aren't you? Because of what I said to you earlier? Why are you sweating like that? You're transparent, Horace, that's what you are.

HORACE (*perspiring*): Who, me? [*Sets the placard against the rails: the letters "ISM" are stencilled on one side.*]

BARBARA: Is that it? ISM? Whose initials are those?

[*On the table, the cutlery starts to rattle. HORACE rotates the sign from "ISM" to show "DOWN WITH CAPITAL-". The lanterns swing from the canopy. The gangway to the Embankment creaks. . . .The Mikhail B. begins to respond to a great surge from across the Thames.*]

[*Unbalanced on tall heels*]: Horace! We're ADRIFT!

[*She totters; HORACE bends at his knees.*]

Ooooh. Oooooohhhhh!

Oh, oh! Ah, Horace, please let go of me!

[*She says this, but he has not yet touched her. So, he grabs her, then releases her; she falls back against the rails, where it is her turn to cling to the lifebelt. . . The surge subsides.*]

You must learn to control your urg-.

HORACE: - I was only trying to-. -It was a surge - from across the river.

BARBARA   (*regaining her composure*): You mean we're not adrift?

HORACE: No. It was a surge.

BARBARA: Well, we'll say no more about it for now, then.

HORACE (*humiliated*): Yes, of course.

BARBARA (*tight-lipped*): I'll-. Do you smell that? How very strange. I'll swear there's something burning. I'd better return to the galley. [*Excited, crosses to Stage R.*]

[*Once again, HORACE sets about straightening the cutlery.*]

[*BARBARA hesitates*]: -By the way, Horace?

[*HORACE, fork in hand, looks up.*]

Who exactly *is* Mr Shine?

HORACE: Who?

BARBARA: Mr Shine. I heard you say his name; don't deny it.

HORACE: The name came into my head - out of nowhere. Just like that! [*Elated, he snaps his fingers.*]

[*BARBARA shows a quizzical smirk, then descends - slowly, slowly - into the galley. Lights to twilight.*]

SCENE TWO

*In the twilight interval, HORACE restores the settings of the table.
Spotlight as ROBERT GREENE appears at the Stage L. gangway.*

ROBERT GREENE (*pauses at head of gangway*): Ahoy there,
    Horace! Request permission to come aboard?

HORACE: Permission granted, Mr Greene.

   [*Cut spotlight; restore lights.*]

   [*THE LAWYER and the MERCHANT BANKER also appear
   at the head of the gangway. Behind them again, a distraught
   DR SAXXE-COBURG tags along.*]

HORACE (*reaching at a wayward spoon*): Welcome on board,
    gentlemen. Take your places, if you please.

   [*The LAWYER and the MERCHANT BANKER are eager to
   get started. Not so DR SAXXE-COBURG, whose face is a
   deep shade of grey. HORACE escorts the three men to the
   Stage R..-end of the table, where they are seated. Downstage,
   HORACE reaches to rotate the placard from "DEATH TO
   CAPITAL-" to "ISM". Then HORACE produces a notebook,
   takes the guests' orders for aperitifs and prepares the drinks
   at the service area.*]

ROBERT GREENE: Where's Mrs Foxxe this evening, Horace?

HORACE (*serving*): Mrs Foxxe? In the galley, sir.

LAWYER: In the galley?

MERCHANT BANKER: You're joking?

HORACE: No, gentlemen, I don't tell jokes on duty. Mrs Foxxe is
    preparing dinner, which will be served shortly.

ROBERT GREENE: Where's the staff this evening?

HORACE: Tonight, she *is* the staff, Mr Greene.

> [*In the distance, there is a roar of disapproval, which quickly subsides.*]

DR SAXXE-COBURG: A complex system reduced to Unity. In this instance, a dual Unity. I can see it all now.

LAWYER: Well said, Herr Doctor. Are you - ah, well?

DR SAXXE-COBURG: Now, I shall return to Vienna.

MERCHANT BANKER: I wish I were going with you, Herr Doctor.

ROBERT GREENE: You know, Horace . . .on a night like tonight, on a boat like this, a man like you could prove very useful. I'm sure my learned companions would agree.

> [*MERCHANT BANKER and the LAWYER - reluctantly - nod their heads in agreement. DR SAXXE-COBURG stares into outer space.*]

HORACE: You're the second person tonight who's said something like that to me, sir.

ROBERT GREENE: Oh, really? Well, then, it must be true.

> [*The men at Stage R. raise their glasses - yes, yes, yes. In the near distance, there is a disturbance.*]

MERCHANT BANKER: They're getting closer.

LAWYER: Who's idea was it to come down here, anyway?

HORACE: You needn't worry, gentlemen; if there's any trouble, we'll put out to sea.

> [*The guests look even more worried. HORACE turns, and disappears Stage R.*]

[*At the head of the gangway Stage L., JAMES BEAM appears with GEORGE FOXXE, who waves grandly from his wheelchair.*

JAMES BEAM wheels GEORGE FOXXE down-stage of the dining table, so that, when positioned, he faces upstage. The men greet each other with smiles, mutters, and expressions of concern.]

JAMES BEAM (*is seated*): I'm not sure it was a good idea or a bad idea coming down here, George.

[*GEORGE FOXXE shrugs, and grins. He appears sedated.*]

Too early to say? Well, maybe you're right. [*Looks along the table.*] You managed to get through all right, gentlemen?

ROBERT GREENE: No problem at all, Professor Beam. I just - walked through - with these gentlemen in tow.

JAMES BEAM: They must have recognised you, then.

ROBERT GREENE: A peaceful demonstration. Nothing to be alarmed about.

[*The MERCHANT BANKER and the LAWYER exchange doubtful glances. DR SAXXE-COBURG is oblivious.*]

JAMES BEAM: Well, maybe they recognise natural authority when they see it. It must be that suit.

[ROBERT GREENE *looks at his own electric-blue suit, but does not respond. . .GEORGE FOXXE looks at the chinese lanterns - happy with this "river world" away from the captivity of the studio.*]

Found your voice yet, George?

[*There is no reply.*]

I guess not.

MERCHANT BANKER: How did *you* get through, Professor?

JAMES BEAM: Let's just say we walked and talked our way through . . .They were suspicious of the wheelchair at first, but we got through, all right.

LAWYER (*amazed*): You mean, you wheeled Mr Foxxe all the way down here - on foot - from The Arms?

JAMES BEAM (*proudly*): I was on foot. His lordship was in the chair.

> [*GEORGE FOXXE grins pleasurably at the achievement. He is, though, fighting against the influence of the drugs.*]

ROBERT GREENE: Coming down Ludgate Hill, you must have taken them by surprise.

> [*GEORGE FOXXE nods his head: yes, yes, yes. . . HORACE's head appears from behind the service area parapet.*]

JAMES BEAM (*surprised*): When you're ready, Horace.

HORACE: Right away, Professor. [*HORACE fixes two more drinks; then he crosses the stage to serve the new arrivals. GEORGE FOXXE clasps HORACE's arm with gratitude.*]

GEORGE FOXXE (*takes a sip, which gives him voice*): Welcome to the Mikhail B., gentlemen. This is my birthday, and you're all invited. Three days early, it's true, but at my age - what difference does it make?

> [*The three men at the far end of the table do not know what to say. A firework goes off in the distance.*]

JAMES BEAM: I'll drink to that.

HORACE: This is Mr Greene - the Deputy-Deputy Mayor. These gentlemen you already know, Mr Foxxe. Dr Saxxe-Coburg, soon to return to Vienna. . . [*Returns - as though to Vienna - to service area.*]

GEORGE FOXXE (*in good humour*): He looks as though he's already gone . . .And - a banker and a lawyer together? I smell trouble. [*Intrigued*]: And you, Mr Greene, I know your boss. I knew Errol when he was a bus conductor. A man of the people, then and now.

[*HORACE grins from ear-to-ear.*]

ROBERT GREENE: I've heard that rumour, too, Mr Foxxe, but only today.

GREENE FOXXE: I wasn't reporting it to you as a rumour, Mr Greene; it's a true fact.

ROBERT GREENE: It's not a widely known fact, then.

GEORGE FOXXE: It is at The Arms. [*Across stage*]: We know everything at The Arms, don't we, Horace?

HORACE: Almost everything, Mr Foxxe.

[*The men at the table - except ROBERT GREENE - laugh.*]

JAMES BEAM: How many deputies does Mayor Flynt have exactly?

ROBERT GREENE (*affronted*): He only has one deputy. Under her, I am one of five. . . Without portfolio.

[*The LAWYER and the MERCHANT BANKER guffaw.*]

ROBERT GREENE: Laugh while you may, gentlemen. My promotion is likely to come through any day now.

LAWYER: You talk of promotion - at a time like this?

MERCHANT BANKER: Shouldn't you be at your desk, Mr Greene?

[*There is a long pause.*]

ROBERT GREENE: I'm an observer at ground-zero. As for Mayor Flynt, I am his eyes and ears. Even this, I shouldn't divulge, but since we are all on this boat together-.

LAWYER: Eyes and ears, maybe; but it is the body of the Mayor the people want.

MERCHANT BANKER: You have not been elected Mr Greene; it is Errol Flynt who should face the public. Where is he?

ROBERT GREENE: At the Assembly - he's, ah, preoccupied.

LAWYER: And I can guess what with - whoever she is. The Mayor's policy choices are clear: brunette, blonde, redhead.

MERCHANT BANKER: The Mayor's body, it seems, is already spoken for.

[*The LAWYER and the MERCHANT BANKER exchange lascivious sneers and guffaws.*]

GEORGE FOXXE: It seems, too, that I've invited you all for dinner - so let us dine! There'll be no discord at my table.

[*The men Stage R.-end of the dining table, thus chastised, nod in agreement.*]

Now, gentlemen, here we all are on the river. A night to remember. We drink, we talk - and, if you like, we *observe*. This is the first time, though, I've brought my own chair to *this* particular event. . .My God, look at it: London by night.

[*A rogue flare explodes over the dome of St. Paul's, illuminating the riverboat deck.*]

GEORGE FOXXE: Is that flame I see - or a reflection of some nightlight? [*Looks to Stage L. Embankment.*] I lost my first wife, you know, to-?

[A *great blast of noise - BUUUURRRRRGH! - emits from the klaxon of a passing barge. After a pause, there is a surge: the glass and cutlery rattle - the chinese lanterns swing - and the barge has passed.*]

ROBERT GREENE: Your wife, Mr Foxxe?

GEORGE FOXXE: You remember, don't you, Horace?

HORACE: Yes, Mr Foxxe - I remember.

GEORGE FOXXE: It was a night like this, wasn't it?

HORACE: It was a night very like this, Mr Foxxe.

JAMES BEAM: If you'd rather not talk about it, George, then don't.

GEORGE FOXXE: I'm sure these gentlemen would be interested to know, wouldn't you, gentlemen? There's nothing like the misfortunes of others to cheer the cynical hearts of over-promoted office workers. Did I say that?

[*The men at the far end of the table cannot believe what they are hearing.*]

I shouldn't have said that, but it just came out. So, I lost her to the flames. What do you think of that? I was away on a business trip. I told her to take the night off - and come with me. Everyone should take the night off on a night like that. Except, Horace, of course. He's like a bat: he never takes nights off. Forgotten how.

Ah, the burden of memory, how it weighs heavy on a man's shoulders.

[*The guests all nod in agreement.*]

Horace, what's that you've got there?

HORACE: I found what I was looking for, Mr Foxxe - the cigars. That old barge must have dislodged the box from wherever it was hidden.

GEORGE FOXXE: Excellent, Horace. After dinner, then, we'll show *THEM* how to make smoke! [*Pauses, thinks.*] Talking of old barges, where's that sister of mine?

JAMES BEAM: They're probably making their way down from the Savoy now, George. That Mr Grey didn't seem like the quitting type to me.

GEORGE FOXXE: He's doesn't know *when* to quit, that's why. He was the one - you know - they sent into Pyongyang that time to-. A grizzly business. This (*looks around him*) is amateurs' night in comparison.

[*ROBERT GREENE looks unsettled.*]

Well, it's history now. Young Mr Greene here is dead right: we should all laugh while we can.

[*The men at the table do not laugh, but they drink deeply, while a thirsty-looking HORACE watches. In the distance, there are screams and shouts. A whorl of grey smoke pumps up into the night sky above Saint Paul's. The drinkers hesitate, and set their glasses down - one by one - on the table.*]

MERCHANT BANKER: They're getting closer. What do you say, Mr Greene?

ROBERT GREENE (*looks upstage*): I don't say anything. Why ask me?

JAMES BEAM (*looks at canopy*): these lanterns'll attract them.

ROBERT GREENE: Those are people out there, Professor - just like us - not moths.

GEORGE FOXXE (*with a smile*): Gentlemen, it is *we* who are the moths. [*Looks up at the canopy.*] These lanterns, too, will draw my sister, - a Queen Moth on a dark night - all the way from New York.

DR SAXXE-COBURG (*remotely*): Do you think they'll get through?

GEORGE FOXXE: She'll get through, Herr Doctor. She's from New York, you know; nothing will stop her. Nothing. Not even-.

[*Above St Paul's, the whorls of grey smoke intensify. MR SHINE appears Stage L. at the head of the gangway. In his red blazer, he surveys the deck. Time freezes. In the distance, the smoke and sparks turn into blue flames of memory.*

A young woman in a white frock for high summer appears at MR SHINE's side; this is EVA FOXXE. A group of five tourists appear - all attired in summer fashion. After a pause, MR SHINE steps onto the deck, but it is EVA FOXXE who leads the way to Stage C., while the group of tourists edge after MR SHINE.]

MR SHINE: Thank you for escorting us down here, Mrs Foxxe. [*Facing Stage L, to the group*]: I'm quite sure I would have lost my way. On this occasion, the guide is guided. Don't tell anyone, and nor shall I.

[*The group teeters - and titters, politely - across the deck to Stage-C.*]

EVA FOXXE (*dreamily*): On the contrary, Mr Shine: my husband is away on business, so I've decided to join your tour. *I* should be thanking *you*.

[*MR SHINE looks upstage, and beams - delighted: he is almost floating on air with the pleasure of the moment. .*

.EVA FOXXE, with her back to us, says something that we cannot quite make out.]

MR SHINE: You hear that everyone? After we leave this fine vessel, then it's back to The Arms for a *hot* roast!

[*Bizarrely, the group provides EVA FOXXE with a round of light applause: she curtsies, deftly.*]

EVA FOXXE: The chef has the night off, I'm afraid, and I'm new to the kitchen, but I'll do my very best for you all! My, what a lovely warm evening it is! Only - I hope I don't burn the place down, ha, ha!

[*Suddenly, no one is listening, as the group and the guide look to Stage R. across the river.*]

Why, Mr Shine, you look lost to the world! [*Moves towards Stage R, such that the lifebelt is visible downstage. MR SHINE, distracted, looks to where she* was *standing, then at where she* is *standing.*].

MR SHINE: Ah, there you are. [*Dreamily*]: Yes, that's it, I'm the guide - who's lost to the world.

[*The group closes to form a huddle at Stage C.*]

EVA FOXXE (*her face glowing*): What's on your mind, Mr Shine?

MR SHINE: Well, Eva. [*Looks through her at Stage L.*] I may call you Eva-?

EVA FOXXE (*glances upstage*): Why not? - no one else does.

MR SHINE (*nervously*): Yes, yes, of course. You know-. I have the strangest feeling I have stood on this deck before.

EVA FOXXE: That's not possible, Mr Shine. . . My husband acquired this vessel only last month - from a Russian émigré - I forget his name just now. He Anglicised it - whatever it was - to Baker, anyway. Mr Baker, Mr Baker, the-. There's a cabin boy that came with the boat. Horace. He's around here somewhere. I've asked him to stay up at The Arms, but he prefers his cabin here on the boat. . .

MR SHINE (*aghast*): Is that usual? Isn't he-?

EVA FOXXE (*businesslike*): A stowaway? An illegal alien?

MR SHINE: I don't know anything about boats, Eva, but I know a good deal about aliens.

EVA FOXXE: - I'm sure that you do, Mr Shine!

MR SHINE (*looks downstage at lifebelt*): And the name - the Mikhail B . . .?

EVA FOXXE: Since it's part of the tour, I can tell you that-.

[*MR SHINE casts his eyes, embarrassed and upstaged, at the deck.*]

The boat, according to my husband - or the émigré vendor - is named for the infamous Revolutionist - Mikhail Bakunin!

MR SHINE (*his eyebrows shifting*): I see. I see. [*To the group*]: Well, there you have it, ladies and gentlemen. Thank you for that, Mrs Foxxe. In that case, you're quite right: I cannot have set foot on this deck before. [*Looks at the group*]: And I'm sure you good people weren't expecting so much excitement in one evening, were you? Well, the night, as they say, is still young - unlike your humble guide. Now, ladies and gentlemen, there's a particularly fine aspect of the Thames to be had at this hour. If we can all now - (*moves Stage R.*) - move along to the Starboard Side, you will see-.

EVA FOXXE (*following*): -Port side, Mr Shine!

MR SHINE (*reaching Stage R.*): Yes, of course. I lost my bearings there again, didn't I? Some guide I've turned out to be!

EVA FOXXE: Careful there, Mr Shine, don't lose your footing: it's a long, long way down!

[*MR SHINE disappears, followed by EVA FOXXE. The group of bewildered tourists has been left behind. In a huddle, they traverse Stage R. - and disappear, one by one, through the bulkhead . . . MR STOKER lingers, and looks at DR SAXXE-COBURG.*]

MR SHINE (*off-stage*): Come along, Mr Stoker, don't get left behind!

[*MR STOKER takes one more good look at DR SAXXE-COBURG, and disappears Stage R.*]

MR SHINE (*reappears*): Is that you, Herr Doctor?

DR SAXXE-COBURG (*stands*): No, it's not me.

MR SHINE: We've been expecting you. Join the tour. Your time is up. Your day has gone - forever.

DR SAXXE-COBURG: No, no, I was only passing through.

MR SHINE: *We're* all only passing through, Herr Doctor. Come along now; your wife is waiting for you.

DR SAXXE-COBURG: My wife? She's dead. She's-.

MR SHINE: Now, there's no need to be like that, Herr Doctor. This way, please. [*Disappears.*]

DR SAXXE-COBURG: I'll be right here, Mr Shine.

[*DR SAXXE-COBURG, his face chalk-white, is forced to consent. Passes towards Stage R. and disappears. . . In the distance, the blue flames and grey whorls of smoke subside, and the view - as before - transforms to the orange glow around Saint Paul's.*]

ROBERT GREENE (*unfreezing*): Did anyone feel a draft just then?

HORACE: Didn't you know, sir, that-?

GEORGE FOXXE: -Now, now, Horace, you mustn't frighten our guests with your stories.

ROBERT GREENE: I don't believe in things like that.

JAMES BEAM: Oh no? Then, what *do* you believe in Mr Greene?

ROBERT GREENE: I believe that the world is made up of real, tangible objects - material things. People are chained by their superstitions - or outlandish promises of - ah, the paranormal life - while advanced materialists harvest what does not belong to them from under our very noses . . .What I mean to say is, -.

JAMES BEAM: I think you've said it.

ROBERT GREENE: - Ah, by the way, WHERE is Dr Saxxe-Coburg?

LAWYER: Vienna?

[*LIGHTS to twilight.*]

SCENE THREE

The lights fade further, and the set darkens - except for the lantern lights suspended from the canopy and - in the background - the glow around Saint Paul's dome. Against the noises of the river, HORACE moves out from behind the service area with a lighted taper. He stides along the length of the table - lights each candle in turn - and withdraws to the Stage-R. service area. Darkness settles over the river. At the service area, HORACE has turned on a desklamp, which illuminates the control panel. HORACE, with this power at his fingertips, smiles and lifts his eyebrows in a conspiratorial way. . . Then, in the downstage distance, flames erupt into flashes. At the dining table, the men's faces are illuminated. . . There are shouts in the distance - followed by a pop-pop-pop of gas capsules - and then there is silence. . .As the scene progresses, the lighting remains subdued, with the occasional flare going off in the background. . .HORACE, to calm the guests, fiddles with his control panel, and sweet violins - Montovani! - play in the background.

GEORGE FOXXE: It looks as though we're about to be boarded, gentlemen. My God, it's-.

> [*At Stage L., a boarding party makes its way along the gangway.*]

CARLTON GREY: We were lucky to get through alive.

MARGARET FOXXE (*off-stage*): We were lucky to get through at *all*. . .Dreadful, *dreadful* people. And all at the State's expense, no doubt. [*Coughs.*] The insurance companies won't be caught-out on this one, my dear Carlton.

CARLTON GREY: Awful haircuts.

MARGARET FOXXE (*off-stage*): I agree, Mr Grey - a haircut and a bath is what's needed.

CARLTON GREY: Who for?

MARGARET FOXXE: Why, *you*, Carlton, *YOU*! I've never seen you in such a pickle!

[*The boarding party step onto the deck:. . .ELAINE WICHELL wears a shabby black cocktail dress and old-fashioned spectacles. MARGARET FOXXE (who is "well-worn") wears an expensive red cocktial dress cut for a dowager . . .CARLTON GREY's expensive suit is beginning to look ragged with perspiration and extended travel.*]

CARLTON GREY (*looking back*): Well, if they've been trying to make a point, I think they've made it.

MARGARET FOXXE (*looks upstage*): I have the feeling, Carlton, they haven't finished making their point just yet. [*Turns*]: Ah, my dear brother - there you are!

GEORGE FOXXE: Welcome on board; I knew you'd find us, somehow. Gentlemen my sister - Margaret.

MARGARET FOXXE: We searched the length of this river - what's it called? - looking for you.

CARLTON GREY: The Thames, Margaret. It's called the Thames.

MARGARET FOXXE (*turns*): This way, Elaine!

ELAINE WICHELL (*looks Stage R.*): Did you see-? Did you see that man in the red blazer? [*Turns, with a winsome face.*] He was leading those people along the river there.

MARGARET FOXXE: I, for one, saw no such thing, Elaine.

GEORGE FOXXE: Are you going to join us, or not?

[*The men at the table stand, and - one by one - are reseated like automatons.*]

ELAINE WICHELL (*peers upstage*): He looked like a tour guide of some kind.

MARGARET FOXXE: Really, Elaine, in *these* circumstances? Do tourists watch things like that. . .? One day, your imagination will take you some place - and you'll *never* come back!

[*MARGARET FOXXE moves across stage; she pretend-kisses her brother on the head - he winces - and she is seated beside JAMES BEAM.*]

Gentlemen, good evening. [*She nods at each in turn with much gravity. She glances at ELAINE WICHELL and CARLTON GREY in turn; they are seated at the Stage L.-end of the dining table.*]

My travelling companion, Miss Elaine Wichell; my Advisor, Mr Carlton Grey. You may recognise *him.*

Well, George, don't you have anything to say for yourself?

GEORGE FOXXE: We were hoping not to attract the wrong kind of people. Looks like we're out of luck. [*Cackles.*]

MARGARET FOXXE: Very amusing, I'm sure. . . I see you're in our Granddaddy's wheelchair. Any particular reason?

GEORGE FOXXE: Well, he doesn't need it any more - that's for sure. But I'll tell you anyway, Maggie: Just the other day I was in my studio; I came over faint, and sat down. After a while, I noticed I was in the wheelchair. When I tried to get up, I couldn't.

MARGARET FOXXE: Oh phoo-ey!

GEORGE FOXXE: It seems the old boy won't let me go! [*Pretends to struggle; invisible arms hold him tight.*]

ELAINE WICHELL: It's true, Margaret.

[*All heads turn.*]

Your brother is being held - at The Arms.

MARGARET FOXXE: Whatever do you mean, Elaine?

> [*CARLTON GREY, distracted by the violin music, looks up at the canopy.*]

ELAINE WICHELL: You know, there's something about this boat that-. It *floats* in a certain way.

MARGARET FOXXE: -Not now, Elaine, please.

ELAINE WICHELL: Well, I'm sorry, Margaret, but the feeling came over me just then, when-. No - no - I've lost it.

MARGARET FOXXE: Elaine-.

ELAINE WICHELL: It was here, but now it's gone. Now, you have my full attention, Margaret. [*Smiles in a fay way.*]

GEORGE FOXXE (*brings his face closer to a candle*): Your travelling companion, did you say? Please inform Miss Wichell that I won't have that kind of thing on this boat.

MARGARET FOXXE: Please, George, don't *taunt.*

> [A *great, silent tongue of flame erupts over the dome of St Paul's, but no one seems to notice, except for HORACE, who looks up from his service area.*]

ELAINE WICHELL (*ethereally*): *Taunt*, did you say?

MARGARET FOXXE (*to the table*): My third husband used to taunt - all the time. By sheer coincidence, he was called Mr Fox, with one X. I merely restored the second X and the final E of my maiden name, and so here I am today.

GEORGE FOXXE (*grinning*): Fully restored?

MARGARET FOXXE: On the subject of husbands and wives, I understand there's been a new addition to the family? Quite a surprise, I must say. Ah, where is she, George?

GEORGE FOXXE: I don't recall. I've been cooped up. Why, these last days have passed in a kind a haze. The fog of the Thames has passed through my head, sister. Smoke or fog, I don't know the difference any more. Then again, who does?

MARGARET FOXXE: You see, Elaine? I ask a simple question, and-.

GEORGE FOXXE: - That, sister, was not a simple question. I think I've been doped.

JAMES BEAM: You're not serious, George?

GEORGE FOXXE: I don't know if I'm being serious, Jim.

MARGARET FOXXE: How do you mean *doped*, George? You're not on any medication, are you?

GEORGE FOXXE: Not as far as I'm aware. Unless someone's slipped me a Mickey Finn. My throat, it's on fire. [*Takes a drink.*]

MARGARET FOXXE: Well, who would do such a thing?

ELAINE WICHELL: That's it, don't you see, Margaret?

GEORGE FOXXE (*to his sister*): Is your companion all right?

ELAINE WICHELL: I'm perfectly all right, Mr Foxxe. I was wondering if I might enquire-?

GEORGE FOXXE: Enquire away.

ELAINE WICHELL: Has there ever been - a *fire* on this boat?

GEORGE FOXXE (*eyes wide*): Only in the boiler room.

ELAINE WICHELL: That's not quite what I meant-.

GEORGE FOXXE: I know what you meant, Miss Wichell. The answer is no.

ELAINE WICHELL: If not a fire, then the intention of a fire - is on this boat.

GEORGE FOXXE: I'm not sure I follow your drift, young lady.

[*HORACE reappears on the deck.*]

Horace! I thought you'd gone overboard!

HORACE: Who, me, sir?

GEORGE FOXXE: Yes, you, sir.

[*HORACE moves about the stage with a tray of fresh drinks. At one point, he appears to interrupt a private, three-way argument between ROBERT GREENE, the LAWYER, and the MERCHANT BANKER.*]

MARGARET FOXXE (*aside*): Horace. Could this be the same Horace-? The boy who-?

ELAINE WICHELL: It's all so confusing here: I can't quite tune-in the way I normally do. It must be the vapours of the river.

MARGARET FOXXE: Well, then, don't try. [*Faces HORACE*]: Mr Horace Baker, is that you?

HORACE (*stands downstage*): It *is* me, Mrs Foxxe: a pleasure to see you again, and you Miss Wichell, and you, too, Mr Grey.

MARGARET FOXXE: You still live here on the boat, Horace?

HORACE (*embarrassed*): Ah, yes, Mrs Foxxe, some of the time. Always, in fact.

GEORGE FOXXE (*muses*): Tonight, Horace. We need you at The Arms tonight, for sure.

[*HORACE is non-committal.*]

ELAINE WICHELL (*to MARGARET FOXXE's ear*): Ancestral memory: someone is trying to get through.

GEORGE FOXXE: We were the one's trying to get through, Miss Wichell, and we did, didn't we, Jim? From the hill to the river.

JAMES BEAM (*proudly*): We certainly did, George.

MARGARET FOXXE (*stunned*): You rolled down the hill? In our Grand-daddy's wheelchair? Tell me you're joking, George. Please.

GEORGE FOXXE: No joke, Maggie! Victory, I say!

MARGARET FOXXE: I ought to hold you responsible, Professor.

JAMES BEAM: I acted on impulse.

MARGARET FOXXE: The two of you? At your age? Down that hill in the face of-? I can hardly believe it. We'll speak about this later. As for victory, which victory are you talking about?

GEORGE FOXXE: I'll take any that's going, sister. Why not? I've had acres of defeat in my time.

MARGARET FOXXE: I hadn't realised defeat was measured in acres.

GEORGE FOXXE: All right - hectares, then.

MARGARET FOXXE: Victory against what exactly?

ELAINE WICHELL (*aside*): Don't you see it, Margaret?

GEORGE FOXXE: Well, let's see now. . . [*Eyes his sister*]: The Conglomerate, for instance.

MARGARET FOXXE: Oh, them.

GEORGE FOXXE: Yes, them. It. They have agents everywhere.

MARGARET FOXXE (*disturbed*): Agents? You mean *here* - in our midst?

GEORGE FOXXE: You think the Conglomerate is imaginary? Like Miss Wichell's tour guide with the red blazer?

ELAINE WICHELL (*charmed*): You saw him, too, then?

[*Belowdecks, a saucepan-lid clatters in the galley.*]

MARGARET FOXXE: What was that? [*Listens.*] . . .Do you sense anything, Elaine?

[*Long pause.*]

ELAINE WICHELL: I sense. I sense - nothing. Oh - it's moved along the riverbank there . . .. No, it's gone . . .East.

[*MARGARET FOXXE provides ELAINE WICHELL with a look of enormous, withering patience.*]

MARGARET FOXXE: The idea of relaxing in London for a few days may have been ill-*advised*. [*She glances at a reflective CARLTON GREY; then looks downstage at the smoke and the flames in the distance.*]

GEORGE FOXXE: I've never known you to relax, Maggie. I thought you came all this way to satisfy your curiosity. It must be eating the heart out of you.

MARGARET FOXXE: That's no way to talk in front of the guests, George.

GEORGE FOXXE: Why not? They're not listening.

[*The argument at the Stage R.-end of the table continues to unfold.*]

Horace, when these gentlemen reach a conclusion, let me know.

HORACE: Yes, Mr Foxxe. I think they've almost finished now, sir.

MARGARET FOXXE (*to ELAINE WICHELL*): The sooner we move on for Paris, the better.

GEORGE FOXXE: We're safe here on the boat. If there's any trouble, we'll put out to sea. [*Looks Stage R.*]   Right, Horace?

HORACE: Right you are, Mr Foxxe. But-. The Frothblowers, sir?

MARGARET FOXXE: I'm sure there's no need for that kind of thing, George.

GEORGE FOXXE: The Frothblowers? What about the Froth-blowers?

HORACE: They've made a booking for this evening. I'll have to return to The Arms later on, sir.

MARGARET: There - you can't put out to sea, George, without Horace.

[*ROBERT GREENE, the LAWYER and the MERCHANT BANKER interrupt their argument to show interest. . . JAMES BEAM and CARLTON GREY confer on a matter of mutual interest.*]

GEORGE FOXXE: It seems we may have some additional guests, everyone. Horace, remind everyone - including myself - who the Frothblowers are exactly?

[*HORACE has disappeared; he returns from the galley with a great serving dish of soup.*]

Ah, there you are, Horace.

[*HORACE moves across the stage, and starts serving - at high-speed - with a ladle. The guests - except ELAINE WICHELL - are amazed by his athletic skill.*]

I was asking - about these Frothblowers?

HORACE (*between places*): A group of gentlemen from the City. This is their big night out. An advance booking, Mr Foxxe, if you recall. Mrs F-.

GEORGE FOXXE: -Now, I remember. Well, maybe they'll cancel.

HORACE: I don't think so, sir. [*Reaches Stage-L- end of the table - serves.*] I've heard it said that the Frothblowers stand aside for nobody.

CARLTON GREY: Artichoke?

GEORGE FOXXE (*surprised*): You're with us, then, Carlton?

MARGARET FOXXE: How extraordinary. These Blowers sound like one of those secret societies.

ELAINE WICHELL: Frotherblowers, Margaret.

GEORGE FOXXE: Mr Greene? You heard of these fellows?

[*ROBERT GREENE shakes his head; as does the LAWYER and the MERCHANT BANKER.*]

MARGARET FOXXE: My - ah, *first* - husband was a member of the Grand Order of Buffaloes, you know. I know - through *bitter* experience - all about this kind of thing. [*To ELAINE WICHELL*]: He used to wear this enormous great furry hat on certain occasions.

[*CARLTON GREY casts his eyes - despairingly - at the canopy; and then - with a start - seems to think one of the chinese lanterns is on fire.*]

Said it belonged to an old Indian Chief from Dakota. Can you imagine that, Elaine, a full-grown man wearing a thing like that?

ELAINE WICHELL: The Chief?

MARGARET FOXXE: No, girl, my first husband. Whenever he wore it, I wouldn't speak to him. Not a word. [*Looks at her brother*]: Don't say it, George.

GEORGE FOXXE (*smiling*): I wasn't going to say anything, Maggie.

MARGARET FOXXE: You're not a Buffalo, are you, Professor?

JAMES BEAM: No, Mrs Foxxe, I'm not a Buffalo. Or an Elk.

[*MARGARET FOXXE, mightily relieved, rests back in her seat.*]

GEORGE FOXXE: Well, everyone - enjoy your soup.

MARGARET FOXXE: Isn't a certain someone going to join us?

GEORGE FOXXE: A certain someone? Sure, Horace - as this is a special occasion - join us.

MARGARET FOXXE: I meant a certain new wifey? Is she . . . unwell? A headache, perhaps, brought on by the disturbances in the neighbourhood? Elaine is simply *dying* to meet her.

ELAINE WICHELL: I am?

MARGARET FOXXE: Yes, dear, you *are*. [*To her brother*]: Well, brother, where is this *wonderful* new wife of yours?

GEORGE FOXXE: My guess is she's in the galley.

MARGARET FOXXE: You mean-? [*Outraged, but pleased*]: In the galley! You've sent your new wife to the galley?

[*Turns*]: Is that right, Horace?

HORACE (*straight-faced*): Yes, Mrs Foxxe. Mrs Foxxe is in the galley.

MARGARET FOXXE: You mean, she's a prisoner?

HORACE: No, Mrs Foxxe, you're thinking of the brig. I mean, Mrs Foxxe is in the galley - the kitchen.

MARGARET FOXXE: Please don't tell me what I'm thinking, Horace.

HORACE: No, of course not, Mrs Foxxe.

MARGARET FOXXE: I know what I'm thinking. And I know what a galley is, Horace.

HORACE: Yes, of course, Mrs Foxxe.

GEORGE FOXXE: She supervising herself, then. Dinner will be served shortly. [*Parenthetically*]: I've been meaning to say that for a while now.

MARGARET FOXXE: And the staff? What's happened to the staff?

GEORGE FOXXE: Well, Horace is here.

MARGARET FOXXE (*leans forward*): George, I know Horace is here. I've just been talking to him. I mean, the rest of the staff. [*Reposes.*]

ELAINE WICHELL (*stands up, abruptly*): I'll go help in the galley!

MARGARET FOXXE (*startled*): You'll do no such thing, Elaine! You're needed *here*!

[*ELAINE WICHELL is reseated, disappointed.*]

[*The three men - ROBERT GREENE, the LAWYER, and the MERCHANT BANKER - appear to be planning a revolt. They become unsettled, exchange whispers, and are ready to make their move. HORACE has his eyes on them.*]

Well, George?

GEORGE FOXXE: Well what? [*Considers*]: I'm sure she'll join us when she's ready. [*Turns to see ROBERT GREENE standing.*] Mr Greene, why are you standing? You don't like your soup?

[*ROBERT GREENE looks at the LAWYER and the MERCHANT BANKER; both renege.*]

ROBERT GREENE: I have business ashore. You're right; I should, really, be doing something about all of this.

JAMES BEAM (*to the women*): Mr Greene's with the Mayor's Office.

GEORGE FOXXE: It's dangerous. Stay here on the boat. Please, Mr Greene, be seated.

[*There is a wolf-like howl from the Embankment; ROBERT GREENE is persuaded, and sits to confront this soup.*]

That's better. [*Aside*]: For a moment there, I thought we had a mutiny on our hands.

MARGARET FOXXE: Well, I don't know what to say, George, I really don't.

GEORGE FOXXE (*in good-humor*): You'll think of something, Maggie.

[*A glorious blaze begins to develop in the vicinity of Saint Paul's. There are shouts in the distance . . .There is an almighty thunderflash downstage - near the Embankment -*

and ELAINE WICHELL leaps to her feet - to reveal a shapely figure.]

MARGARET FOXXE: Oh, really, Elaine! Please try and calm yourself!

[*ELAINE WICHELL, realising the danger has passed, resumes her position at the table.*]

You've been on-edge ever since-.

ELAINE WICHELL: Yes, I know, Margaret - ever since last year in New York.

MARGARET FOXXE (*addresses the table*): It was a fine summer's day - rather like today - and Elaine was on her way to my apartment. [*To JAMES BEAM*]: And guess what happened?

JAMES BEAM: I don't know: what happened?

MARGARET FOXXE: She was caught up in a demonstration. A riot, if you like. You've always been a high-strung girl, haven't you, Elaine?

ELAINE WICHELL: The demonstration was high-strung, Margaret.

MARGARET FOXXE: But, really, to be arrested as an-.

JAMES BEAM: Arrested? Why, that's unbelievable. Whatever for?

MARGARET FOXXE: There were others, Professor, of course-.

[*ELAINE WICHELL glances along the table, and seems to show faint recognition of ROBERT GREENE, who sits up, uncomfortable in his chair.*]

JAMES BEAM: Others? Which others?

MARGARET FOXXE: What *was* it they called you, Elaine?

ELAINE WICHELL (*head bowed*): They said I was an - (*pronounces demurely*) - agent *provocateur.*

MARGARET FOXXE: Can you believe it, Professor? A slight, harmless girl like Elaine: an *agent provocateur*?

GEORGE FOXXE: Harmless, did you day?

[*There are murmurs along the table; ROBERT GREENE shows fresh interest in ELAINE WICHELL. A mite drab when she first appeared, she begins to glow under the attention. She removes her spectacles, for good, in favour of her in-built radar.*]

MARGARET FOXXE: Fortunately, I am acquainted with the Commissioner of Police.

ELAINE WICHELL: I was *hoping* they'd let me go because I was *innocent!*

MARGARET FOXXE: Anyway, this summer we decided on Europe. First stop, London. A change of scene for the poor girl.

JAMES BEAM: A change of scene, did you say?

MARGARET FOXXE: Well, in the circumstances, perhaps not.

GEORGE FOXXE (*after a pause*): That's about the best pre-dinner antidote I've heard in years. An *agent provocateur?* Well, I never.

ELAINE WICHELL: I can assure you, Mr Foxxe, I am no such thing.

MARGARET FOXXE: Pay no attention, Elaine, George is a tease - a natural, born tease. Why, when I was a girl-.

GEORGE FOXXE: -When you were a girl, Maggie, Teddy Roosevelt was in short trousers.

MARGARET FOXXE: You see? He just can't help himself.

[*There is another thunderflash downstage - more light than noise. Again, ELAINE WICHELL is onto her feet.*]

Now, now, Elaine! - There's no need for-! [*Looks downstage, unsure.*] . . .alarm.

ELAINE WICHELL (*standing*): How do you know there's no need for alarm, Margaret? You don't know!

[*CARLTON GREY, roused somewhat by the flash, offers her a comforting arm, and she reseats herself at the table.*]

MARGARET FOXXE: That's no way to speak, Elaine. [*Turns*]: Why are we having dinner on here - on the Mikhail B. - and not at The Arms?

GEORGE FOXXE: It's my birthday.

MARGARET FOXXE: It's not your birthday. I'd know if it were your birthday.

GEORGE FOXXE: It's not safe on Fleet Street

CARLTON GREY: I'm inclined to agree, George.

GEORGE FOXXE: There. See? Your advisor is inclined to agree. After all these years, he's finally realised the shareholders are not worth dying for.

[*The three men at the end of the table applaud. There is a surge from some craft passing on the river. The chinese lanterns hanging from the canopy begin to sway.*]

MARGARET FOXXE: Shareholders?

CARLTON GREY: We're on vacation.

GEORGE FOXXE: My sister and her companion are on vacation. You, on the other hand, are a strategic investor - and strategic investors are never on vacation. [*Turns.*] Carlton Grey is here to cut a deal; you can be sure of that. I can see it in his eyes. There's grey steel there, all right. Probably on your behalf, Maggie. . .

MARGARET FOXXE: Please, George, *don't.* The Arms won't have a future unless-. [*Swallows her words.*] Carlton knows how to *leverage-*.

GEORGE FOXXE: You think he can face up to the Conglomerate? This is a different kind of battle, sister, than he's used to; if you ask me, Carlton does not seem himself. Then again - who, does? Now, let is consider the soup: it gets colder.

[*CARTON GREY reaches for his soupspoon; the rest of the guests follow his lead.*]

Well, Carlton, you have something to say?

CARLTON GREY (*spoon-pause*): The asset value of The Arms has realised considerable growth; as a going-concern, however, its prospects are in terminal decline - without new management. And even then-? Risky. A disposal might be advisable. [*Continues spooning.*]

GEORGE FOXXE: He doesn't say much, but when he does - you know something's been said. You hear that everyone? I'm to be disposed of.

MARGARET FOXXE: Not you, George dear, The-.

GEORGE FOXXE: - I'm to be pushed, so it's George, *dear.* Enough! Jim, maybe we should return to The Arms to see if it's still there!

MARGARET FOXXE: I agree: it ought to be safer there.

ELAINE WICHELL: I don't think it's safe *anywhere.* I have a feeling about that.

JAMES BEAM (*respectfully*): You do, Miss Wichell? What kind of feeling, exactly?

ELAINE WICHELL: That man over there: he's up to something, I'm sure of it.

[*A spotlight appears at Stage L. - and sweeps across the deck to Stage R.*]

[*Spooked*]: What's that light?

GEORGE FOXXE: River Police, that's all . . . .[*Watches, listens. Waves Stage R. as the River Police vessel passes.*]

[*The spotlight wavers in the vicinity of Stage R. First, it hovers on ROBERT GREENE - it shows him up for what he is - as the shell of an empty blue suit! - then, it darts towards HORACE, who is revealed at a control panel, where his hands work at switches and buttons. At downstage, various flashes and thunderclaps go off in quick-fire succession, while HORACE grins like a madman. The spotlight hesitates, and moves off-stage R.*]

HORACE! ARE YOU ALL RIGHT OVER THERE, HORACE?

HORACE (*drops hands to his sides*): Who, me, sir?

GEORGE FOXXE: Yes, you, sir. Is that dinner I smell from the galley?

LAWYER: Smells like CS gas to me.

BARBARA (*off-stage, belowdecks*): HORACE! HORACE!

[*HORACE looks down the flight of steps leading belowdecks.*]

BARBARA (*offstage*): We're running late, Horace.

HORACE: Yes, Mrs Foxxe. Shall I-?

BARBARA: Please announce that dinner will be served.

HORACE (*his face illuminated by the hatchway*): Yes, Mrs Foxxe.

> [*HORACE reaches for a dangling sash above his service station, and rings the bell for dinner.*
>
> *Lights to dark. Candlelight and the chinese lanterns illuminate the tableau. The violin music rises, reaches a flourish, and then fades into the background.*]

S C E NE FOUR

Lights as before. In the background, the dome of Saint Paul's is illuminated by an emergency services' spotlight. In near-silhouette, HORACE and BARBARA move back and forth between the service area and the dining table. After an interval, everyone appears replete. In the background, even the rioters seem to be having a break.

At one of the candles, someone is lighting a cigar: GEORGE FOXXE smokes with relish. The general lights are restored. The diners are slumped back in their seats; several bottles of claret have been consumed. Only ELAINE WICHELL is alert; she is perched on the edge of her seat, watching the host puff-puff at the cigar.]

MARGARET FOXXE: I was hoping to have a word, Barbara.

BARBARA: The galley, Margaret, beckons! [*Exit Stage R.*]

ELAINE WICHELL (*canopy gazing*): What *wonderful* lanterns, Horace! Are they imported?

HORACE (*turns on a heel*): Yes, Miss Wichell, by F.W. Woolworth.

ELAINE WICHELL: Oh.

> [*HORACE returns to the service area. At the control panel, he flicks a few switches, which seem to let off damp squibs at water level. He smiles, satisfied, as - downstage - a blue flare shoots up into the sky, then drifts on a tiny parachute - slowly, gracefully - over the river beyond Stage R.*]

GEORGE FOXXE (*after a puff*): Well done, Horace.

HORACE: (*turns*): Thank you, sir.

ELAINE WICHELL: Enjoying your cigar, Mr Foxxe?

GEORGE FOXXE: Why, I haven't had a cigar since-. [*Frowns, loses his way.*]

ELAINE WICHELL: Yes, I know, Mr Foxxe. Since-.

GEORGE FOXXE: You do? How do you know?

ELAINE WICHELL: I feel that I do. Now you're going to ask me when I was born. After that again, you're going to ask me what brought me to London.

GEORGE FOXXE: This conversation is becoming a trifle one-sided, don't you think?

ELAINE WICHELL (*smiles*): I knew you were going to say that, too, but I thought I'd not mention it.

> [*ROBERT GREENE seems to have become entranced by ELAINE WICHELL; he declines his companions' offer of a second escape attempt.*]

JAMES BEAM: Are you quite all right, Miss Wichell. Perhaps-.

ELAINE WICHELL: There's no need to be concerned, Professor. The truth is - despite what Margaret may have intimated - there's not much wrong with my nerves. There are - rather -

disturbances in the outside world, which are reaching the interior world - beyond. . .

[*MARGARET FOXXE glances at her companion.*]

 I need them - my nerves, don't you see? - for my particular line of research.

[*ELAINE WICHELL appeals to GEORGE FOXXE, who resists comment. Then she turns to look at JAMES BEAM.*]

JAMES BEAM: I'm not going to ask, either.

ELAINE WICHELL I've heard it said that there are a lot of - ah, ghosts - along Fleet Street.

GEORGE FOXXE: Fleet Street *is* a ghost, Miss Wichell, that much is true. The Arms is in the way, too - of development - it seems. And she flew across the Atlantic - my own sister - to make it happen.

MARGARET FOXXE: I, George, did not *fly* across the Atlantic. [*Pouts*]: I took an airliner. . .And now that I'm here, your new wife proves elusive. I had my suspicions at first, but now I see she's no more than a galley wench to you. So, how *was* the honeymoon?

GEORGE FOXXE: The honeymoon was protracted and difficult. I've only this day emerged from my studio, and begin to see the light. I've been a captive inside my own skull. Thanks to the Jack of Clubs - and the Professor here - I'm free. You say let's go back to The Arms, when I'd just as well never see the place again. [*To CARLTON GREY*]: An asset, is that all it is?

MARGARET FOXXE: What ever do you mean by all that, George? Why can't you talk straight, like everyone else?

GEORGE FOXXE: Like you, Maggie . . .?

MARGARET FOXXE: You judge your only sister too harshly.

GEORGE FOXXE: Anyway, there you have it. [*Blows a big plume of smoke at one of the chinese lanterns, which sways in response.*] Horace? [*Looks across stage R.*] . . . Please convey my thanks to Barbara for an excellent dinner.

[*HORACE takes a step towards the telephone extension.*]

Not now, Horace - later.

[*HORACE falters behind the service area; he stands, stiffly.*]

Now, Horace, you can relax.

[*HORACE's shoulders slump slightly inside his penguin suit.*]

Not by that much. [*Puffs cigar; again, he hits the chinese lantern with the plume.*]

[*HORACE straightens his shoulders.*]

MARGARET FOXXE: Oh, please, George, don't taunt. You're taunting again.

ELAINE WICHELL: Taunt, did you say?

GEORGE FOXXE: Who, me?

MARGARET FOXXE: So, you're better - after days of captivity, or so you claim - and you're up to your old tricks already. You always were a trickster, George . . .[*Looks downstage*]: All of this . . .is probably one of your elaborate tricks - to amuse yourself.

GEORGE FOXXE: If it makes you feel better, Maggie, then go ahead and think what you will, but you give me too much credit - for too little.

MARGARET FOXXE: Isn't he, Elaine? He's taunting poor Horace who's been on his feet since eight this morning.

HORACE (*from across the stage*): That's six o'clock, ma'am.

MARGARET FOXXE: Oh all right - six - then. What difference does it make?

JAMES BEAM: I calculate: about two hours.

GEORGE FOXXE: If they were your feet doing the standing, Maggie, you'd know the difference, all right.

MARGARET FOXXE: You see, Elaine? This is a boat-load of old tricksters. *Tricksters*, I say, for whom playing it straight would be-.

ELAINE WICHELL (*on some other plane*): - Anathema?

MARGARET FOXXE (*concerned*): Who? Elaine, are you *with* us? I ask again: are you with us, dear?

ELAINE WICHELL (*looking up at a lantern*): Just, then, I-.

CARLTON GREY: She's hypnotised by the lantern. It had to happen - sooner or later.

MARGARET FOXXE: Elaine, Elaine . . .?

ELAINE WICHELL: - I felt it . . .Someone -. No, not someone, a group of them . . . walked over my-.

JAMES BEAM (*to GREY*): This happened before?

> [*CARLTON GREY nods that - oh yes - it's happened before, all right.*]

MARGARET FOXXE: You've had a terrible fright, you poor girl.

JAMES BEAM: Jet lag, that's what it is.

MARGARET FOXXE (*glances dubiously at JAMES BEAM*): Brandy, is what you need now, Elaine. Come to think of it, I think I'll join you.

GEORGE FOXXE: Well, Horace usually- . Horace! If you please, brandy for Miss Wichell.

> [*ELAINE WICHELL turns, and discovers that HORACE has already crept across the deck; he is standing behind her with a decanter of brandy at the ready.*]

ELAINE WICHELL: OH! There you are, Horace. How did you-? Oh, never mind.

GEORGE FOOXE: The gentlemen at the end, Horace - they look like they need it. Courage, eh?

> [*HORACE approaches the Stage R.-end of the dining table; the MERCHANT BANKER relieves him of the decanter. . .In the distance, there is a satisfied roar: the rioters are making progress - towards the Mikhail B.*]

BARBARA (*belowdecks*): HORACE! HORACE!

> [*MARGARET FOXXE's head - her hair piled high - emerges from a bulkhead at Stage R. Puffs and blasts and jets of steam shoot out from around her head - as from the overheated galley. Aghast, ELAINE WICHELL looks across the stage at this apparition.*]

HORACE (*takes a step back*): Yes, ma'am . . .?

BARBARA: Your soup, Horace, is ready. Artichoke, your favourite

HORACE: My favourite is asparagus.

BARBARA: That's what I meant, Horace; there's no need to split hairs.

GEORGE FOXXE: Wha-? Is that you, Barbara?

MARGARET FOXXE: We haven't seen much of her, have we? [*Looks at Stage R.*] We don't see much of her *now*. . . [*Turns, looks at ELAINE WICHELL, who is spellbound by the lantern*]. Oh dear, oh dear.

BARBARA: Yes, George. I'm almost done: I mean, we can't let Horace starve, can we?

GEORGE FOXXE: Are you starving, Horace?

HORACE: More or less, sir.

GEORGE FOXXE: Barbara: fetch him some the soup, if you please.

[*At Stage R., the head of BARBARA withdraws slowly into the void. The puffs of steam subdue into wisps, and then nothing . . . HORACE does not know which way to turn.*]

HORACE: Mr Foxxe, I would prefer - I mean, I think it would be more appropriate if I dined . . .*alone.*

[*There is an awkward silence.*]

What I mean to say is-?

GEORGE FOXXE (*puffs gingerly at his cigar*): -I know what you meant, Horace. And what *I* mean to say is this: you'll have your soup on deck with the rest of us if that is okay with you, sir.

HORACE: Yes, Mr Foxxe.

MARGARET FOXXE: Really, George, I don't know why you taunt the poor fellow. Why, there's a side to you that-. You're a slave driver, dear. How your first wife lived with you, I really do not to this day understand.

GEORGE FOXXE: -That'll do, Maggie.

[*HORACE has taken on the appearance of a relic; an automaton, he crosses the stage to the galley steps, accepts a plate of soup from a pair of white hands, and returns to the dining table. He seats himself beside ROBERT GREENE, and waits.*]

MARGARET FOXXE: The poor girl. You kept her in the kitchen, too, and you knew she wasn't qualified.

GEORGE FOXXE: Who? Oh. Well, it was a long time ago. Sometimes, I wonder if it ever really happened.

MARGARET FOXXE: I'm sorry, George. It was a dreadful thing to happen. She was such a *darling* -.

[*ELAINE WICHELL, picking up on some antique memory waves, becomes wide-eyed but speechless.*]

GEORGE FOXXE: So you say: but I seem to recall you didn't approve of her, *either*. You're the one who said she *belonged* in the kitchen

MARGARET FOXXE: Really? I have no memory of ever having said that. But one thing's for sure: if she married you for your money, the poor girl certainly *paid* for it.

GEORGE FOXXE: She wasn't like that; you've got it all wrong.

MARGARET FOXXE: She must have fallen for your natural charm, then.

GEORGE FOXXE: I don't want to talk about it.

ELAINE WICHELL: A memory - gone up in smoke.

[*Cigar-smoke pours from GEORGE FOXXE's mouth as he stares at ELAINE WICHELL.*]

MARGARET FOXXE: And the one in the galley? Is she like that? Why didn't you tell the family you were to re-remarry? And at your age, too. Why the secrecy? You *are* married, aren't you, George?

GEORGE FOXXE: I don't know; I suppose I must be. No more brandy, Maggie. You've had your say.

ELAINE WICHELL (*dreamily*): Polyamnesia, that's what it is.

CARLTON GREY: That's in the South Seas, isn't it?

GEORGE FOXXE: Enough, enough.

> [*ROBERT GREENE, the MERCHANT BANKER, and the LAWYER all watch HORACE - waiting form him to commence eating the soup. HORACE drops the spoon into the plate with a clatter, making ELAINE WICHELL jump.*]

MARGARET FOXXE: Well, Mr Greene, what has the Mayor's Office got to say? Is London always like this?

> [*ROBERT GREENE fails to respond; he is under ELAINE WICHELL's spell.*]

GEORGE FOXXE: Normally, Maggie, there's much more traffic, and not so many pedestrians lined up behind makeshift barricades.

> [*MARGARET FOXXE looks upstage, befuddled; then she looks along the table.*]

MARGARET FOXXE: I *had* wondered. [*Along the table*]: Mr Greene, do I understand correctly? The Mayor's Office has nothing to say on this subject? Mr Greene-?

ELAINE WICHELL (*remotely*): I see a great deal of confusion surrounding our Mr Greene.

> [*ROBERT GREENE is exposed by the remark.*]

MARGARET FOXXE: Elaine, please. I'm sure Mr Greene is a very nice man who is not at all confused.

ELAINE WICHELL: That's not what I meant.

MARGARET FOXXE: You're *not* confused, Mr Greene, are you?

ROBERT GREENE: Only by your companion, Mrs Foxxe. [*He is beguiled by ELAINE WICHELL.*]

BARBARA (*appears at Stage R.*)*:* Horace, where are-. Oh, there you are.

MARGARET FOXXE (*looks across the stage*): Ah, there you are, my dear. Isn't it time we had our little chat?

BARBARA: Not now - if you don't mind - Margaret. I'm in need of Horace.

[*MARGARET FOXXE casts her eyes at the deck.*]

GEORGE FOXXE (*to BARBARA*): As this is a special occasion, I've asked Horace to join us.

[*HORACE has not touched his soup; with all eyes on him, he makes a reluctant start.*]

BARBARA: The dishes-.

GEORGE FOXXE: -The dishes will keep; they always do.

[*Everyone there - except HORACE - seems to agree.*]

MARGARET FOXXE: Join us, Barbara; you'll work yourself into an early grave in that galley.

BARBARA: Since you put it that way, Margaret-. [*Crosses to Stage L.-head of the table and is seated In BARBARA's presence; ELAINE WICHELL seems to transform; she smiles, wickedly, and a black lock of hair hangs around her shoulder.*]

ELAINE WICHELL: Having a good time, Barbara?

BARBARA: In the galley? I'm having a *great* time, Elaine.

[*JAMES BEAM pours BARBARA a drink.*]

Why, on a night like this, I could-.

ELAINE WICHELL: Yes. . ?

BARBARA (*looks into ELAINE WICHELL's dark eyes*): Nothing.
   Really.

MARGARET FOXXE (*to BARBARA*:): There - peace in our time   -
   at last. Listen. Silence over the-.

CARLTON GREY: -The Thames, Margaret.

MARGARET: Yes, Carlton I know it's the Thames . . .

   [*Everyone listens: there are no shouting rioters, flares or
   passing boats. . . A sense of peace - serenity even - pervades
   the deck. The chinese lanterns swing against a light breeze.
   The water laps-lap-laps against the hull of the Mikhail B.
   Then - the silence is interrupted by another kind if lapping -
   a loud slurping noise. It is HORACE at his soup, his right-
   elbow cocked, as he spoon-paddles his way into the soup
   plate.*]

HORACE: Slurp, slurp . . .*SLURP*!

   [*ROBERT GREENE, the MERCHANT BANKER and the
   LAWYER grin like schoolboys.*]

MARGARET FOXXE: Really, George, can't you do something?

GEORGE FOXXE: You said he was starving, Maggie. You were
   right!

MARGARET FOXXE: Does he have to eat his soup like that?

GEORGE FOXXE: I don't know; I'll ask him. Horace, do you have
   to eat your soup like that?

HORACE (*oblivious*): Slurp, slurp . . . *slurp*.

MARGARET FOXXE: George, do we *have* to listen to this cacophony?

HORACE: SLURP!

GEORGE FOXXE: All right, Horace: that'll do for now: you've made your point - whatever it is!

HORACE (*pauses, looks up*): I have, Mr Foxxe? Right you are, sir. [*Continues spooning, quietly.*]

MARGARET FOXXE: Now, where were we. . ?

CARLTON GREY: You were saying how peaceful it was around here, Margaret.

[*MARGARET FOXXE provides CARLTON GREY with a slow, steel-cutting gaze.*]

I didn't mean that the way it sounded, Margaret.

[*There is a growing clamour in the distance.*]

ELAINE WICHELL: I have a feeling that-.

JAMES BEAM: What, again? What kind of feeling is it this time, Miss Wichell?

ELAINE WICHELL: The kind of feeling, Professor, I haven't had for a long time. It's like molasses flowing through my veins.

MARGARET FOXXE: Whatever is it, Elaine?

ELAINE WICHELL (*alarmed*): Also, a feeling that . . . we are . . about . . . to be . . . BOARDED!

MARGARET FOXXE (*jumps*): Boarded? [*Accidentally knocks over a wineglass.*] Oh!

HORACE: SLURP!

[*BARBARA has eyes only for HORACE's bizarre soup-eating performance. . .The approaching clamour is now punctuated by distinct shouts.*]

THE MOB (*from down-stage*): Fascists! Bourgeois bleeding bar-stewards! SCUM!

CARLTON GREY: Who's calling who scum?

[*The boat begins to rock in its berth. Objects fall from the sky, onto the canopy, so that the chinese lanterns swing crazily.*]

MARGARET FOXXE: You said we were safe here, George!

GEORGE FOXXE: I meant *comparatively*.

MARGARET FOXXE: Comparatively safe? What on earth does that mean!

GEORGE FOXXE: It means, Maggie, that maybe I was wrong.

[*ELAINE WICHELL's eyes flutter - making contact - and she goes into a dead faint.*]

MARGARET FOXXE: ELAINE!

[*JAMES BEAM quickly moves around the end of the table; ELAINE WICHELL slumps - out cold - into his arms.*]

JAMES BEAM: She fainted.

MARGARET FOXXE: Is that all you can say, Professor? You understand these things. Why don't you *do* something?

JAMES BEAM (*his hands full*): What do you want me to do?

[*ROBERT GREENE, THE LAWYER, and the MERCHANT BANKER stand up from the table, and retreat Stage R, then downstage. CARLTON GREY is onto his feet.*]

CARLTON GREY: No you don't! [*He crosses the stage.*] I've had me eyes on you three for some time. I know a deserter when I see one - or three. RATS!

MARGARET FOXXE: Aren't *any* of you going to do anything? Carlton, where are you going? Leave those poor men alone!

BARBARA: Horace! For God's Sake, stop your slurping!

MARGARET FOXXE (*to BARBARA*): I don't think it matters now, dear, do you?

HORACE: Yes, ma'am. [*Slurps away.*]

[*A group of thugs - about five of them to begin with - appear at the head of the gangway at Stage L.*]

THUG #1: There they are! Greedy capitalist pigs! Look! That one there! Stuffing his face, he is! A proper little gentlemen, ain't 'e?, sucking his soup!

THUG #2: He's not the one! He is! The geezer in the silver suit! [*Points at CARLTON GREY, who has cornered the three men against the rails. The MERCHANT BANKER and the LAWYER - absurdly - fight over the lifebelt, while ROBERT GREENE gauges the distance to the Embankment.*]

NOW!

[*The group of thugs, with a war-cry chorus, charge down onto the deck. Then the group, still acting in concert, freezes!*]

BARBARA (*turning*): They're going to kill us all!

[*The dinner guests freeze. Next, the sound of - more thugs? - move up the gangway at Stage L. Instead, MR SHINE and his group appear at the head of the gangway.*]

DR SAXXE-COBURG: Ah, just like the old days.

MR SHINE (*looks over his shoulder*): Everyone still with us? Herr
Doctor? Miss Ashe? Is that you down there, Mr. Stoker?
[*Turns, steps onto the deck.*] I don't know how, but we seem
to have come full circle. Never mind; now that we're here, I
might as well tell you the story . . .[*The rest of the group step
off the head of the gangway - one by one- and stand in a
huddle around MR SHINE. They are oblivious of the frozen
group of thugs and dinner guests. MR SHINE, obscured by
his group, pushes his way through the huddle to stand
upstage.*]

That's better. Now, where was I? Yes. There was, I'm *afraid*
to say, an unfortunate incident here at the turn of the century.

MISS ASHE: Unfortunate? Incident? What do you mean, Mr Shine?

MR SHINE (*patiently*): I was coming to that. You won't faint, Miss
Ashe?

MISS ASHE: No, I don't think so: not now, anyway.

MR SHINE (*rubbing his hands gleefully*): The story is that a group
of well-heeled dinner guests were beaten to death here.
There was not the time, even, for dessert - before they met
with their fate.

MR STOKER: You have a ghoulish sense of humour, Mr Shine, if I
may say so

MISS ASHE: Who by, Mr Shine?

MR SHINE: Who by, indeed, Miss Ashe? You may well ask.

MISS ASHE: Well, I *am* asking . . .

MR SHINE: Anarchists, I believe. Or a group of thugs who
happened to be passing.

MR STOKER: Anarchists? Here in London?

MR SHINE: Oh, yes, Mr Stoker: you would be surprised what's in the woodwork waiting to come out. [*MR SHINE peers upstage.*] They're everywhere these days. Waiting for their time.

MISS ASHE: But we're not talking about these days, Mr Shine, are we? The turn of the century, you said.

MR SHINE (*exposed*): Yes, I did say that, didn't I?

MISS ASHE: Yes, you did. It's one of your tour-guide stories. I think you're trying to frighten us.

MR SHINE: You don't think I'd do that, do you, Miss Ashe? [*Gazes at her, frighteningly. MISS ASHE recoils.*] . . .So, here our wealthy friends were - some of them Americans, it's true - enjoying a beautiful summer evening on the Thames, and-. Well, as I've already said. . .They were boarded, and that was that. The boarding party is said to have been particularly angered by what the saw as a particularly bourgeois group. Oh dear, of dear, what a world we live in. . . [*Looks at the deck, depressed, and places his hands in the blazer pockets.*] The leader of the group - after he was arrested - said that the bourgeoisie have power, but not the will to do right by it, such that - therefore, it is not real power - only the semblance of power-. Oh dear. He himself came for a middle-glass home, you see, so he knew all about that kind of thing. He's a Member of Parliament now. His name escapes me for the moment. Mr Gre-.

MR STOKER (*confused*): -Class, you mean. You said middle *glass* home.

MISS ASHE: You make is sound like he lived in one of those new high-rises.

MR SHINE: I did? They didn't have those then.

MR STOKER: Yes, you did.

MR SHINE: Well, I meant *class*. [*Annoyed.*] Of course I meant
class. . . Anyway, anyway, this is not really part of the tour. I
don't know what's come over me. I'm distracted, that's what
it is. [*Laughs, nervously.*] I think, perhaps, we should all be
on our merry way. So, to conclude. [*Takes in a deep breath
of Thames air.*] One of the guests, who was not a guest, but
a member of staff, and not so well heeled, put up a
courageous stand, but in the end . . they were all drowned.
Most unfortunate.

MISS ASHE: *All* of them, Mr Shine? Beaten, you said, not
drowned.

MR SHINE: Beaten, then drowned. As I say, Miss Ashe, most
unfortunate.

MR STOKER: And who did you say was responsible, Mr Shine?

MR SHINE: Events; the tide of history, Mr Stoker.

MR STOKER: I'm not sure I follow you, Mr Shine.

MR SHINE: Class War; the Mob. People set higher standards for
other people than do for themselves. I've noticed that.
[*Resigned*]: So, they always come - sooner or later -. [*Looks
around at what he perceives is an empty deck.*]

MR STOKER: Well, there's nothing we can do about it, Mr Shine,
is there?

MR SHINE: I don't know, Mr Stoker; I'll have to give that some
thought. . .Now, perhaps we had better be on our merry way.

MISS ASHE: We're *with* you there, Mr Shine.

[*Ushers his group up the gangway and off Stage L.*]

MR STOKER (*reappears at Stage L.*): Smells like someone's left
the soup on. [*Turns, disappears into the night.*]

[*The action on the deck unfreezes: HORACE continues at his soup spooning, The five thugs pounce on CARLTON GREY. In the rush, GEORGE FOXXE is upended in his wheelchair, and collapses downstage of the dining table, where he drags the tablecloth and cutlery with him to the deck - with a CRASH!*]

MARGARET FOXXE (*stands*): George! George? Is that you under there?

GEORGE FOXXE: Of course, it's me. Who the hell else-?
BARBARA (*stands, moves upstage*): Horace! HORACE!

HORACE: Slurp! [*Calmly*]: Yes, Mrs Foxxe?

BARBARA: Save us!

HORACE: As you wish, Mrs Foxxe. [*Sets his spoon down with a clang, wipes his lips with a napkin. . .. From the Stage L. gangway, another group of rioters sprawl onto the deck, and set upon MISS WICHELL, who is unconscious, and JAMES BEAM, whose hands are full. The rioters surround the dinner guests - except for ROBERT GREENE, the LAWYER and the MERCHANT BANKER. In the downstage distance, London is on fire: there is an explosion - a petrol tank - and a cascade of flares: ROBERT GREENE is exposed by the light against the downstage railings, and leaps onto the Embankment.*

In the middle-downstage of the chaos, BAKUNIN, THE WILD MAN appears: at first, he seems to be with the thugs, but then - on a whim - turns against them, with swinging fists and boots, so that his coattails flail through the air. At one point, he seems to perform a somersault for the fun of it, and then, as though jumping on a trampoline, he lets out a yell, and seems to bounce downstage - across the river.

HORACE takes over: he takes a step towards the downstage rail: he snatches the Mikhail B's lifebelt from the railings, shoves it over the head of the nearest thug - like a necklace - and pushes the confused youth over the rails, and into the water with a SPLASH!   There are cheers from the Embankment, at which HORACE waves acknowledgment. The remainder of the thugs - aware of HORACE's power - begin to retreat. HORACE stoops, reaches for the deck, and grabs a long bargepole. Once positioned, he charges across the Stage R-L with it, such that the last of the boarding party are pushed up, onto the gangway at Stage L, and out of sight: three bodies fall into the water - splash - splash - SPUR-LASH.

The MERCHANT BANKER and the LAWYER see their chance, climb overboard, and follow ROBERT GREENE's lead.

CARLTON GREY's suit is left in tatters and his hair is in spikes. ELAINE WICHELL now seems to be sleeping in JAMES BEAM's arms. GEORGE FOXXE, trapped in his wheelchair under the tablecloth, groans.

BARBARA and MARGARET FOXXE, ignoring the old man under the table, stare at HORACE, amazed.

HORACE still holds the barge pole, ready to rebuff any further boarders.

CURTAINS CLOSE on a scene of devastation.]

ACT III

CURTAINS. LIGHTS. The Arms: later that evening. In the distance, visible through the observation window, the various fires around St Paul's have settled into a steady blaze of flame, sparks and - occasionally - a billow of black smoke. . .The riverboat dinner party has succeeded in finding an escape corridor from the Thames back to Fleet Street. Positioned at various locations - the group is recovering from its ordeal.

GEORGE FOXXE is resplendent his wheelchair - now battered and scraped - at Centre-Stage. JAMES BEAM is at his side on a stool. ROBERT GREENE stands at Stage R. and moves across Stage L. where he sits in the cubicle by himself.

At the Centre-Stage table, MARGARET FOXXE and ELAINE WICHELL are seated with CARLTON GREY who watches the archway void at Stage R.; his hair is in spiky disarray, and his face is striped with charcoal.

HORACE stands behind the snug bar. BARBARA stands to tend his head wounds.

BARBARA (*dabbing at HORACE's forehead*): Stay still, Horace! I'll dab you in the eye if you don't stop your fidgeting!

[*HORACE grimaces without a sound. BARBARA violently sets his head straight, and dabs more ointment: she appears to be torturing him in her own way. ROBERT GREENE looks on - cold, unsympathetic - while, at the other extreme, ELAINE WICHELL seems to wince every time HORACE winces. In this way, the long table downstage is disused - so that the action is brought upstage.*]

HORACE: Ahhrg!

BARBARA: You sound like an old warthog, Horace! Stop it now!

HORACE: Argh. I can't, Mrs Foxxe: it *hurts*!

MARGARET FOXXE (*aside*): Does he *have* to call her 'Mrs Foxxe'?

GEORGE FOXXE: Any sign of other two, Mr Greene? Hatton and Rose?

ROBERT GREENE: They were headed in another direction.

JAMES BEAM: They were last seen with you.

ROBERT GREENE: No, Professor, you're mistaken; I took a wrong turn - and ended-up . . .back here.

JAMES BEAM: But-.

GEORGE FOXXE: They'll turn up, Jim. I know those two: if I were to announce beer on the house, they'd come walking right through that door there.

> [*Everyone looks at the entrance Stage R., then the portal at Stage L.*]

. . .Well, I haven't made any such announcement, have I?

MARGARET FOXXE: And you never will, George.

ROBERT GREENE: They've probably returned to the suburbs - where they belong.

JAMES BEAM: Maybe they saw something they weren't meant to see, and were made to disappear.

ROBERT GREENE: Like what, Professor?

JAMES BEAM: That's what I'd like to know. When they followed you up that alleyway, they vanished.

ELAINE WICHELL (*distracted*): I see. . . two bodies . . .

MARGARET FOXXE: That's Carlton and myself, Elaine.

ELAINE WICHELL: No, no, not you.

MARGARET FOXXE: Where, then?

ELAINE WICHELL: . . .Floating in the Thames. The two of them: a lawyer and a merchant banker. Pin-striped, belly-up, then face-down in the river - the pair of them.

GEORGE FOXXE: That's Hatton and Rose, all right. Those big, overfed bellies would make the float like that.

MARGARET FOXXE: If you wouldn't mind, George.

ELAINE WICHELL: Evil shows its colour, but not its face. The colour is-.

ROBERT GREENE: She can't know that; she can't possibly know that. There's fifty bodies a year recovered from the river.

JAMES BEAM: Oh, Mr Greene? Then make that fifty-two this year.

HORACE: -Arh. Arg.

GEORGE FOXXE: There's a good fellow, Horace. Next time, we'll take her off-shore a stretch. The boat, I mean.

[*BARBARA interrupts her dabbing - stares daggers at GF - then resumes HORACE's torture.*]

MARGARET FOXXE: Brother, how you can make light of this affair - is beyond me. Look. Look. Look, at poor Miss Wichell!

[*GEORGE FOXXE looks at ELAINE WICHELL, who is - by some transformation - radiant, with her dark, raven hair hanging down around her shoulders . . . She is, however, on some other plane.*]

GEORGE FOXXE: I'm looking. The woman is clearly prone to some kind of suggestion. She looks well on it, though, I must say. As for Hatton and Rose, they've probably gone for a beer or two elsewhere.

MARGARET FOXXE: It's a miracle we got out of there alive - any of us.

ELAINE WICHELL: *Miracle*, did you say . . .?

[*MARGARET FOXXE pats her companion on the wrist.*]

GEORGE FOXXE: No miracle, Maggie: that was Horace's secret escape corridor from the river. Stumbled upon - when he needed it - when he was a boy. Says he couldn't find it again, until tonight - when we *all* needed it. Isn't that right, Horace?

[*HORACE shows an eyeball; he doesn't dare move.*]

ROBERT GREENE: You said the *first* time, Mr Foxxe? When he was a boy? Escaping from what exactly?

GEORGE FOXXE: Says he can't remember.

ELAINE WICHELL: It's that polyamnesia again. It's affecting everyone these days.

GEORGE FOXXE: I hadn't realised they'd reached you, Horace.

HORACE: Not by the boarding party, sir. Afterwards, when I fell down the galley steps. Argh.

BARBARA: Sssh now! Well, unlike some people I could mention, I think Horace has acted very bravely this evening.

HORACE: Ah. Ah. *Ahhhh*.

BARBARA FOXXE: Don't be a big baby, Horace! Stop your fidgeting, and stay *still*!

HORACE (*grimacing*): Yes, ma'am.

ELAINE WICHELL: How far, Horace?

HORACE: How far what, Miss Wichell?

ELAINE WICHELL: How far did you fall?

MARGARET FOXXE: What does it matter how far he fell?

BARBARA: For the person doing the falling, Margaret, I should think it matters a great deal.

MARGARET FOXXE: Please do not speak to me in that way, Barbara. George, tell your-. Oh, never mind.

[*BARBARA finishes with HORACE's head; she turns, and smiles at MARGARET FOXXE.*]

ROBERT GREENE (*curious*): How far, Horace?

HORACE: All the way, Mr Greene - all the bloody way!

GEORGE FOXXE: That'll do, Horace. Remember, these people are our guests - whether we like it or not.

MARGARET FOXXE: There's no need to be like that, brother.

JAMES BEAM: He's been through a lot, George.

GEORGE FOXXE: Yes, I know, Jim.

JAMES BEAM: Why, the way he took on those-. [*Pauses, looks at CARLTON GREY.*] Now that I think of it, they seemed to be after *you*, Mr Grey.

CARLTON GREY (*twists in his seat*): Me? Why would they be after me, Professor?

JAMES BEAM: Well, that suit: I warned you about that earlier. Once they'd boarded, they went straight for you. Didn't seem much interested in anybody else.

CARLTON GREY: Well, I don't know what you're getting at, Professor, but I can tell you this: I don't like it; not one bit.

JAMES BEAM: It was merely an observation.

CARLTON GREY: Then I must ask you to keep your mere observations - to yourself - or confine them to your laboratory.

ROBERT GREENE (*slow handclaps*): Here, here; I think we've had enough of the Professor's *observations*.

JAMES BEAM: This *is* my laboratory, Mr Grey. I told you: I'm on field assignment.

CARLTON GREY: I know all about field assignments.

MARGARET FOXXE: Mr Grey was with the Special Forces, you know. Up the Peninsula.

GEORGE FOXXE: If you ask me, we're all up the Peninsula.

JAMES BEAM: I'm inclined to agree, George. As for Mr Grey, all I meant was-.

ELAINE WICHELL: They were after the fattest wallet, Carlton, that's all; nothing personal.

CARLTON GREY (*reaches for wallet, which is not there*): I think you may be right, Elaine. [*Looks upstage with a blank face.*] I've been fleeced.

[*On impulse, JAMES BEAM reaches for his wallet, which -
his expression shows - is still there. MARGARET FOXXE
cannot resist checking her purse.*]

GEORGE FOXXE: I thought you didn't carry cash, Maggie?

MARGARET FOXXE: No, I don't - ever. Not until-. I only wanted
to see if-. Oh, never mind.

GEORGE FOXXE: 'Never mind,' she says.

CARLTON GREY: I don't know about you good people, but what
I'm going to have is a good stiff drink. One for the road, and
beyond. [*Stands.*] And don't tell me I look like I need one,
Professor, I know - and, to tell you the fact of it, I think I've
passed caring. [*Crosses stage to snug bar.*] Set 'em up,
Horace.

MARGARET FOXXE: So, here we all are. And people accuse me
of being a socialite.

CARLTON GREY: We've moved further to the left than that,
Margaret; we made a successful retreat, which - some
strategists say - is the best form of attack; but now I'm not so
sure. The situation is this, my friends: now that we're here,
how are we going to get out of here? The phone-lines are
dead; an electronic fog pervades the sky.

MARGARET FOXXE: I've never known you so eloquent, Carlton.

CARLTON GREY: It's the drink, Margaret, and I'm not done yet.
The Metro is at a standstill. Fleet Street is blockaded at both
ends. For the time being at least, the authorities seem to have
lost control of the situation. Am I right, George?

GEORGE FOXXE: I don't like to say so, Carlton, but you sum it up
pretty well.

BARBARA: I shall inform Mr and Mrs Cameron immediately.

GEORGE FOXXE: Leave them alone, Barbara; they're better off in their room not knowing.

MARGARET FOXXE: Well, we could all try just getting up - and, ah . . . *leaving*?

ROBERT GREENE: I wouldn't recommend that, Mrs Foxxe.

MARGARET FOXXE: Why ever not, Mr Greene?

JAMES BEAM: He's right, Mrs Foxxe: we're surrounded - for the rest of the night, anyway . . .

ELAINE WICHELL: It'll be the longest night of our lives, Margaret. You wait and - see. [*Distracted, she moves back onto her other plane.*]

MARGARET FOXXE: Carlton, what do you *advise*?

CARLTON GREY: At this stage . . .withdraw and consolidate.

MARGARET FOXXE: It seems clear that we have already withdrawn.

CARLTON GREY (*takes a drink*): All right - consolidate, then.

MARGARET FOXXE (*leans forward*): What do you *advise*, Carlton?

CARLTON GREY (*teases*): How about we draw straws?

GEORGE FOXXE: Good idea. What for?

ROBERT GREENE: We're trapped. Mr Grey is suggesting someone should go outside for help.

GEORGE FOXXE: But who?

JAMES BEAM: Not who, George: *what*. The straws decide.

MARGARET FOXXE: *Out there . . .?*

GEORGE FOXXE: You're the one who wanted to just get up and go, Maggie.

MARGARET FOXXE: That was then; this is now. I am prepared to accept Carlton's good counsel.

ROBERT GREENE: I believe Mr Grey overestimates the danger. That's because danger is attracted to him. It's clear for all to see.

CARLTON GREY: Well, thank you for your support, Mr Greene. Anything I can do for you some time - well, don't ask.

ROBERT GREENE: I am prepared to test that assertion - by volunteering Mr Grey. After all, he's the one they're after.

CARLTON GREY (*incredulous*): The way you phrase that-. *Your* prepared? Well, that's mighty big of you! [*Reflects*]: First rule of the military, Mr Greene: never volunteer.

ROBERT GREENE: Pyongyang?

CARLTON GERY: I don't know how you could know about that. But *that* was different.

ELAINE WICHELL (*descending*): The straws must decide.

GEORGE FOXXE: Horace, the straws.

ELAINE WICHELL: Horace, make sure it's *real* straw.

HORACE: I'll try, Miss Wichell.

MARGARET FOXXE: Really, Elaine, what's wrong with ordinary drinking draws?

ELAINE WICHELL (*ascending*): Drinking straws are made of waxed paper. It has to be *straw*. It won't work, otherwise. Tell him he'll find some - there! - on that Chianti bottle, on that shelf over there ...

GEORGE FOXXE: Horace?

HORACE: Yes, Mr Foxxe, I've got them. [*Locates straw; turns. Prepares strips of straw on the palm of his hand.*]

GEORGE FOXXE: Are those straws ready yet, Horace?

HORACE (*busy*): Almost, Mr Foxxe.

GEORGE FOXXE (*smiles*): Make sure they're all different lengths. We don't want them all to be short straws, do we now?

HORACE (*grins*): No, sir, we don't.

> [*In the downstage distance, a silent gas explosion produces a giant white-and-blue mushroom-cloud of smoke and flame. . . ELAINE WICHELL is transfixed by the vision.*]

MARGARET FOXXE: Elaine, Elaine. [*Shakes her companion's arm.*] Elaine, what have you seen?

ELAINE WICHELL (*snapping out of it*): A vision, Margaret.

MARGARET FOXXE: Of what, may I ask?

ELAINE WICHELL: Oh - (*notices the approaching mushroom cloud, which blasts its way over the roof of The Arms*) - only the end of the world . . .

> [*MARGARET FOXXE, as at some cocktail reception, sits back on her stool, crosses her hands, and regards her companion.*]

JAMES BEAM: That was a close one. I think you've lost your weathervane, George.

GEORGE FOXXE: It won't be the first time, Jim. [*To Stage R*]: You done there yet, Horace?

HORACE: I'm on the last straw now, Mr Foxxe.

[*GEORGE FOXXE smiles, mirthfully.*]

MARGARET FOXXE: You find something amusing, brother, dear?

GEORGE FOXXE: In this situation, I'm prepared to find *anything* amusing.

> [*GEORGE FOXXE looks sideways at CARLTON GREY, who appears to have become gently unhinged.*]

MARGARET FOXXE: After New York, I thought-. Well, I thought we might find some peace and quiet here. . .in London.

> [*GEORGE FOXXE looks, stone-faced, upstage.*]

HORACE: READY, SIR! [*Holds up a fistful of straws.*]

GEORGE FOXXE: You haven't made them all the same length, have you, Horace?

HORACE (*stepping out from behind the snug*): No, Mr Foxxe. There's all sorts here, sir. [*Moves to Centre-Stage. He looks upstage, and holds the straws up in his fist. Then his arm acts like a divining rod, and presents the fistful of straws to CARLTON GREY!*]

CARLTON GREY (*looks up, hound-like*): It's ladies first

MARGARET FOXXE: I can't believe you just said that, Carlton. [*Closes her eyes, opens them.*] Why, you're a changed man, since we retreated from the river.

ROBERT GREENE: He's lost his nerve, that's all.

CARLTON GREY: That's all? For a civilian, Mr Greene, I can see that you like to live dangerously.

ROBERT GREENE: And you *have* lived dangerously.

[*CARLTON GREY is about ready to get to his feet, when HORACE approaches him.*]

CARLTON GREY: Why me first, Horace?

HORACE: It was your idea, sir.

GEORGE: Good for you, Horace.

JAMES BEAM: That boy's got sense.

GEORGE FOXXE: That what's you think.

CARLTON GREY: I've got a better idea.

GEORGE FOXXE: You're not going to suggest we draw straws to see who draws *first*?

MR GREY: No, of course not. Only, I-.

GEORGE FOXXE: Go on - DRAW!

MARGARET FOXXE: George -!

[*HORACE re-presents his fist.*]

CARLTON GREY: All right: but you'll have to keep your hand still, Horace.

[*As CARLTON GREY reaches to select a straw, it is his hand - and not HORACE's - that is shaking, so that it plumps for the nearest straw; he pulls, and has chosen a pip-squeak of a straw. The gathering moans at the sight of the tiny yellow snippet, but everyone - except CG - is relieved.*]

You forced it on me, Horace. You've got to let me draw another!

HORACE: No, sir - with respect, I did not. You forced it on yourself.

CARLTON GREY: George - make your man comply with my wishes.

GEORGE FOXXE: You're not at one of your shareholders meetings now, Carlton.

[*CARLTON GREY clutches at the miniscule straw; he wipes at his sweaty brow. HORACE looks at the investor with something approaching contempt.*]

ELAINE WICHELL (*ascending*)*:* Never mind, Carlton, that one might be *relatively* long.

You never know. Here, Horace, let me have a go.

MARGARET FOXXE*:* Do you think you should, Elaine?

ELAINE WICHELL: *We* all have to, don't *we*? It's the rules.

MARGARET FOXXE: I don't know. I haven't done this before.

GEORGE FOXXE: There's a last time for everything, Maggie.

[*HORACE proffers his fist of straws minus one at ELAINE WICHELL.*]

ELAINE WICHELL: I mean to say, we can't let poor Carlton draw straws all by himself, can we?

MARGARET FOXXE (*bewildered*): Why ever not?

GEORGE FOXXE: That would not be in the spirit of the game, Margaret. [*Turns.*] Would it, Carlton?

MARGARET FOXXE: A game? Is that what this is?

ELAINE WICHELL (*closes her eyes*): Please, Margaret, I'm trying to concentrate. [*Reaches for a straw, and - by a kind of divining - slowly - draws out a long, long straw taper, so that even HORACE cannot believe his eyes.*]

118

[*Opening her eyes*]: Oh! Well, that's a nice one! You see, Margaret, all you need is a little concentration.

MARGARET FOXXE: Here, let me see that!

ELAINE WICHELL (*defensively*): Oh, no - you've got to draw your own.

MARGARET FOXXE: Here, Horace, let me have one of those! [*Snaps at HORACE's fist - pulls out a smallish taper, which she immediately compares with CARLTON GREY's. She relaxes.*]

GEORGE FOXXE (*impatient*): If you take much longer, Horace, those things will be growing out of your hand!

[*CARLTON GREY is alarmed by the prospect, and again checks his miniscule straw. . . .HORACE then moves quickly about the stage, proffering straws in turn, until everyone has a straw . . .HORACE returns to Centre-Stage.*]

Aren't you forgetting someone, Horace?

HORACE: Mrs and Mrs Cameron? I'll go to their room right away, sir.

GEORGE FOXXE: You mean, you'd burst into their honeymoon suite and offer them straws? Horace, you and I must have that little talk one of these days. No - leave them alone: I'm thinking of someone else, entirely.

HORACE: Mr Rose? Mr Hatton?

GEORGE FOXXE: According to Miss Wichell, they're floating in the river. Straw won't do them any good - not now. Now, how many straws remain?

HORACE (*holding up a single, fairly short straw*): One, sir.

GEORGE FOXXE (*smirks*): Then, it's yours.

HORACE (*alarmed*): But, sir, I haven't had a proper draw!
[*Appeals to the group*]: It was the only one remaining!

GEORGE FOXXE: It's yours, anyway. Hard luck, Horace. [*Turns*]:
And speaking of luck, Carlton, it looks like yours has just run
out. Remember this: if you can't join them, beat them.

CARLTON GREY: After all that's happened, what a way to go.

MARGARET FOXXE: You have a wicked, wicked streak in you,
George.

GEORGE FOXXE: After Pyongyang, it'll be like a stroll in the park
to him.

MARGARET FOXXE: You've put Horace up to all these high
jinks, haven't you? You're trying to dispatch us - one by one.
You have a grudge against the society, George, and everyone
in it.

GEORGE FOXXE: It wasn't my idea. [*Turns*]: Was it, Carlton?

CARLTON GREY (*shattered*): Your brother's right, Margaret. It
was my idea. I only meant it as a figure of speech - until
now. [*Stands erect.*] I deserve to go. I ought to go. Anyway,
my tour of duty is done - and I've had enough.

MARGARET FOXXE: WHERE - ARE - YOU - GOING?

[*Outside, there is a rising clamour of voices.*]

CARLTON GREY (*unhinged*): I've got to go. For help. And, while
I'm at it, I think I'll have my suit pressed.

GEORGE FOXXE: That's the spirit, Carlton! These good people
don't know what you're made of, but I do.

MARGARET FOXXE (*rises*): George, you can't let him go out
there!

GEORGE FOXXE (*to the group*): Anyone want to take Mr Grey's place?

> [*Silence. There are no takers. ROBERT GREENE is about to say something, but changes his mind.*]

All right, would the person with the second shortest straw like to take Mr. Grey's place?

> [*MARGARET FOXXE surreptitiously glances at her straw - clearly the second shortest - and sits down without word.*]

ROBERT GREENE: What are his chances, Professor?

JAMES BEAM: Concerned, Mr Greene? I'm touched.

ROBERT GREENE: Interested.

JAMES BEAM: Well, then: it may be safer out there than in here, for all I know. He drew the straw. I can't change that. Anyway, Mr Grey has a mind if his own. Then again, we don't have to go along with a bunch of straws, do we?

ELAINE WICHELL: The straws have decided, Professor. Don't cross them; don't even *think* about crossing them.

CARLTON (*withdrawing slowly*): Yes, right, the straws have decided in their own way. But, I sense an agenda, not set by the straws. In my view, some unknown person or group is manipulating those characters out there to destroy property, not flesh. This suit cost me five thousand dollars, which is outrageous, but I've become attached to it, and - now - it's worth less than ten bucks. My wallet, they already have. It's my theory that they'll vent their anger on the suit, rather than he who's inside the suit. I propose to test that theory.

> [ROBERT GREENE can barely hide pleasure, while *MARGARET FOXXE cannot bear the sight of her advisor.*]

GEORGE FOXXE: Before you go, Carlton. Situation Report?

[*CARLTON GREY finds his resolve, and takes a step Centre-Stage. Spotlight.*]

CARLTON GREY: The Situation Report is as follows. [*Looks upstage*]: I would estimate collateral damage in the range of one hundred to one-hundred-and-fifty millions. The insurance companies - many of which have been hit, and hit hard - are unlikely to prove sympathetic. The cost will fall to government - which since governments do not have any money - means the taxpayer will surely foot the bill. If anything, I predict, for the longer term, increased insurance premiums and an elevation of the business rate. [*Turns*]: It's cheaper than war, George, and it's a way for everybody to let off a bit of steam . . . Oh, by the way, there should be short-term increase in employment in the construction sector, but this will be off-set by a loss of revenue in tourism. That means you, George. [*Bows - cut spotlight - withdraws Stage L.*]

[*At downstage, ROBERT GREENE has a haunted look about him.*]

GEORGE FOXXE: Your conclusion, Carlton?

CARLTON GREY (*stops, turns*): Draw your own conclusion, if you will. But for what it's worth, here's mine: the rich have just got that much richer.

GEORGE FOXXE: That's all I wanted to know. Thanks for the report, Carlton.

[*CARLTON GREY withdraws to Exit Stage L.*]

[*Outside, the city smoulders into the night. HORACE, who is left holding his straw, quickly hides it away. Outside, there is a bloodthirsty cheer. ROBERT GREENE leaps to his feet to peer downstage - through the observation window - and looks onto the streets below. Just then, shreds of a grey suit are tossed up into the sky. Off-stage, the crowd yells HURRAH! HURRAH! - and then silence.*]

JAMES BEAM: See anything, Mr Greene?

ROBERT GREENE: I see a man in jockey shorts. He's running in the direction of the river. He can run, too. I think it's-.

MARGARET FOXXE: Stars and Stripes, Mr Greene?

ROBERT GREENE (*retreats*): I'm not sure. It could be polka dots. It's hard to tell through the smoke. But, if I had to bet on it - why, yes, you're probably right, Mrs Foxxe - Stripes, of some kind.

MARGARET FOXXE: That's our Mr Grey, all right. A patriot to the skin. [*Realises what she has revealed; covers her face.*]

GEORGE FOXXE: It must have been tough, Maggie, for you to let him go.

[*MARGARET FOXXE casts her eyes at the deck, not ashamed, just plain embarrassed.*]

JAMES BEAM: Running around like that, he'll eventually be arrested as a troublemaker. At least then, he'll be safe. I think there's a lesson in that - for us all.

MARGARET FOXXE: Then - when he's arrested - he'll send help. Won't he, Professor?

JAMES BEAM: Eventually, I said. Anyway, why should he help us? We sold him down the river.

ELAINE WICHELL: Do we really need help at all? Why can't we all wait here until things die down?

MARGARET FOXXE: If you thought that, Elaine, why didn't you try and stop Carlton from going outside?

ELAINE WICHELL: I hadn't thought of it then.

MARGARET FOXXE: Oh, really, Elaine, sometimes you make me despair.

[*In the downstage distance, London smoulders.*]

ELAINE WICHELL: It's fate, Margaret. Mr Grey *had* to go out there. If he'd stayed here, he'd end up becoming someone else somewhere else. Don't you see?

MARGARET FOXXE: He became someone else somewhere else years ago. We all did in those days.

GEORGE FOOXE: Whose talking turkey now, Maggie?

ELAINE WICHELL: When he comes back, you'll see, Margaret.

JAMES BEAM: If he comes back alive, that is.

GEORGE FOXXE: He's never missed a shareholders' gathering in his life; he'll be back, all right, for that Extra-ordinary General Meeting.

MARGARET FOXXE: Well, if he was dead, George, he wouldn't *be* coming back, would he?

ELAINE WICHELL: Not necessarily.

MARGARET FOXXE: Now, now, Elaine, let's not have all that again.

ELAINE WICHELL: I only meant-?

MARGARET FOXXE: - I know perfectly well what you meant. Try and get a grip on your nerves before they get a grip on you.

ELAINE WICHELL: There's nothing wrong with my nerves.

[*ELAINE WICHELL sits upright.*]

MARGARET FOXXE: Are you with us, Elaine? Are you?

ELAINE WICHELL: The boat. Das boot is voll.

JAMES BEAM: The boat is full. I know that from somewhere.

MARGARET FOXXE (*to the group*): She's speaking in tongues. [*To herself*]: Oh dear, oh dear. [*To ELAINE WICHELL*]: You think we're in the Alps, is that it? But we're not - we haven't got that far yet. First, Paris; then, Berne. For now, we're here - in London.

ELAINE WICHELL: Are we sinking, Margaret?

MARGARET FOXXE: That, my dear, is debatable. [*Pats her companion's wrist.*] But no, we're not on the boat any more. We're here - safe, I think - at The Arms. [*Looks at her brother*]: Comparatively safe, I mean.

ELAINE WICHELL: Yes, we're afloat. I know that, Margaret. But things - appearances, I mean - are not always as straightforward as that, are they? It's this place. I have a feeling about this place, that-. [*Looks around her at each of the faces of the group.*] It has layers.

GEORGE FOXXE: Not layers - storeys. Six storeys high, not including the basement. [*To his sister*]: I can see where this is leading, Maggie, and I'll tell you again: I won't have it - not on the boat, and not here at The Arms. The two of you'll have to wait until you reach wherever it is you're going for that kind of thing. The whole business gives me the creeps.

MARGARET FOXXE (*intrigued*): Layers, Elaine?

GEORGE FOXXE: That's enough of that. . .

MARGARET FOXXE (*to ELAINE):* What do you mean by layers? Of what?

GEORGE FOXXE: Layers of nonsense, that's what.

MARGARET FOXXE: Do tell, Elaine?

ELAINE WICHELL: I felt it on the boat, and now it's here. There's SOMETHING here, Margaret. Not of our own time, necessarily, but of our own space-time continuum.

GEORGE FOXXE: Is she saying there's spooks in this place? If so, I know that already. I told you, they'd try anything to eject me from this place. I'm an old man who's in the way of progress.

BARBARA FOXXE: George, really, you're becoming suspicious of every body. Even our guests. Even of-. Well.

ELAINE WICHELL: Guests?

MARGARET FOXXE: Guests, Elaine. *Guests.* Not-.

ELAINE WICHELL: That's it. Don't you see? There are guests in this place.

[*GEORGE FOXXE buries his face in his hands.*]

There's something approaching from the East.

GEORGE FOXXE (*almost laughing*): Oh God, no.

MARGARET FOXXE (*wide-eyed*): Now, don't be foolish, Elaine.

[*Outside, over Saint Paul's, the smouldering skyline gives way to fast-flowing whorls of grey smoke - but the phenomenon abruptly ceases to reveal a calm, clear night-sky.*]

George, *do* something. You said we'd be SAFE here. You said it was safe down on the river.

GEORGE FOXXE: For a time, it was . . .

MARGARET FOXXE: You just don't care. You never did.

ELAINE WICHELL: . . .There's - something approaching from the East.

JAMES BEAM: Are we going to start all of that again?

GEORGE FOXXE: Horace, see if that telephone is back on-line.

HORACE (*reaches for the 'phone behind the bar*): Yes, Mr Foxxe.
  [*Picks up receiver, listens.*]

GEORGE FOXXE: Well, I'm waiting, Horace. Still dead?

HORACE (*sets receiver down*): Dead as a dodo, sir. Although-?
  [*Frowns, deeply.*]

ELAINE WICHELL: That's it: a dodo: they're all dead. That's the
  clue I've been looking for!

MARGARET FOXXE: Who's dead?

BARBARA: . . .Although *what*, Horace?

HORACE: I thought . . .I heard a voice asking for Miss Wichell.

  [*ELAINE WICHELL almost floats off her stool.*]

GEORGE FOXXE: And *I* thought you said the line was dead?

HORACE: Yes, Mr Foxxe, but this voice - I must have imagined it
  - it seemed to be inside my head.

BARBARA FOXXE: Who, Horace? Who was inside your head?

HORACE: A Mr Shine. Asking if Miss Wichell is ready to leave
  yet.

  [*ELAINE WICHELL looks about ready to faint; MARGARET
  FOXXE shakes her by the arm.*]

ELAINE WICHELL (*happily, dreamily*): I'll be all right, Margaret,
  I'll be on my way soon.

MARGARET FOXXE: I don't know any Mr Shine, do you, Elaine?

[*ELAINE WICHELL shakes some volume into her dress - and then her hair. With her raven locks around her shoulder, she seems a beauty compared with the frump of earlier. Adjusted, she is ready for departure.*]

You're not to go looking for Mr Grey, Elaine, is that clear? And you're not to go off with this Mr Shine. Somehow, I don't like the sound of that name.

[*ELAINE WICHELL says nothing, MARGARET FOXXE looks at her companion, mystified.*]

GEORGE FOXXE: Horace, you're not losing your marbles, are you?

HORACE (*confidently*): Not a chance, Mr Foxxe.

GEORGE FOXXE: Barbara, perhaps you'd better relieve Horace.

HORACE: I'm all right, Mrs Foxxe, you'll see.

GEORGE FOXXE (*persuaded*): As you were, then, Horace.

HORACE: Yes, sir.   Thank you, Mr Foxxe.   [*HORACE shows enormous relief; he is not crazy, after all.*]

[*BARBARA loses all interest in the the proceedings; she stands to one side with a cockatil glass. Everyone else listens in silence, waiting for the approaching entity. Outside, the night is so dark the dome of Saint Paul's seems to have disappeared.*]

JAMES BEAM (*listens*): I never would have believed it. I think Miss Wichell is right. But - this is approaching from . . .the *West.*

ELAINE WICHELL (*loses her bearings*): My group is approaching from the East, Professor, I'm sure of it.

BARBARA (*noticing*): I don't believe it: the dome of Saint Paul's has disappeared! [*Looks downstage into the night.*]

MARGARET FOXXE (*ignoring BARBARA's observation*): Your group, Elaine? What ever do you mean by that? [*Upstage*]: I don't think I can stand this much longer. [*Turns*]: Elaine, it might not be too late - if we leave *right now*. None of this sneaking out the back way: I mean, straight out the front door - with a vestige of dignity. The staff at The Savoy are probably looking for us at this very moment! We'll meet them half-way!

GEORGE FOXXE: What are you talking about, Maggie? You've never met anyone half-way in your entire life.

JAMES BEAM: You'll never make it. Mrs Foxxe, please reconsider.

[*MF is charmed by the Professor's apparent concern.*]

GEORGE FOXXE: Horace, check that line again, if you would.

[*HORACE lifts the receiver and listens. . .A faint rumble of feet is heard somewhere below Stage R. HORACE rolls his eyes, and then realises the sound is elsewhere. The concert of feet climb the stairwell, and the head of a man appears out of the archway void at Stage R.*]

FROTH BLOWER #1: Not too late, are we? Got held up down the road.

BARBARA (*stands alert*): Oh. I'd forgotten. The booking. George, these are the Froth Blowers. You should let Horace have the rest of the night off. I'll take care of-.

GEORGE FOXXE: I don't know why you would want him out of the way, Barbara, but Horace stays.

BARBARA: Horace has done enough for one night.

GEORGE FOXXE: Horace does not have nights off. Horace, tell her why you do not take nights off.

HORACE: Mr Foxxe always says that the night you take off is the same night something will happen.

[*BARBARA seats herself on a barstool without word.*]

F*ROTH-BLOWER #1 shifts his eyebrows up-and-down; then he steps into the lounge, and is followed by four more FROTH-BLOWERS, who are uniformly attired as businessmen out on the town.*]

GEORGE FOXXE (*looks upstage*): For a moment there, I thought we were in trouble . . .[*Looks Stage R.*] Gentlemen, welcome to The Arms. If it's refuge you seek from the violence, you'll find sanctuary here.

FROTH-BLOWER#1 (*grins, salaciously)*: I wouldn't have put it *quite* that way, sir.

[*The FROTH-BLOWERS - like a group of penguins - head for the snug bar; none of them seem to notice BARBARA.*]

Oh no? Horace, give these - ah, gentlemen   - what they deserve. On the house.

[*HORACE prepares for action.*]

FROTH-BLOWER #1 (*over his shoulder*): You hear that, comrades? That's what I call hospitalization. Now, don't step on that carpet - ah, comrades - you might get carried away. [*Turns*]: Thank you, Mr Foxxe, you're a kindly host . . . Ah, I espie a comely wench and her curmudgeonly maiden-aunt. . . Fair game, is my guess, for a huntsman and his hounds.

[*ELAINE WICHELL shakes her head - no, no, never.*]

FROTH-BLOWER #2: Expecting someone else, ladies?

FROTH-BLOWER #3: Sorry to disappoint you . . .

[*FROTH-BLOWERS #4 & #5 are sizing-up HORACE, who quickly hand-pumps five pints of frothy ale. . . BARBARA sips at a cocktail, satisfied that her allies have arrived at last. All five of the businessmen surround the snug bar like a group of hornets.*]

FROTH-BLOWER #5 (*aside*): Who's the dumb waiter?

GEORGE FOXXE: How do you know about my carpet, Mr-?

[*FROTH-BLOWER #1 peels himself away from the group, and faces Centre-Stage, though careful not to step on the carpet.*]

FROTH-BLOWER #1 (*lighting a cheap cigar):* No names among us, Mr Foxxe: we are the Ancient Order of Froth Blowers, at our service. As for your carpet, all of Fleet Street knows *of* it, but won't step *on* it.

[*Laughter from the group. FROTH-BLOWER #1 glances slyly, lustfully at BARBARA FOXXE: it is clear they are complicit.*]

MARGARET FOXXE (*to ELAINE WICHELL*): We should retire, Elaine. If we can't make it back to the Savoy, then my brother will-.

FROTH-BLOWER #2 (*turning, leaning back against the snug*): - The Savoy, you say? We've just come from there, matron. We started out from Trafalgar Square, and moved up along the Strand and into Fleet Street. It wasn't an easy journey, let me tell you.

MARGARET FOXXE: You're part of the demonstration, then? You're dressed like that to fool the police?

FROTH-BLOWER #2: Oh no, madam. We're not fooling anybody but ourselves. [*Laughter; back-slaps*]. We Froth-Blowers had to fight off a few of them. They were angry, but not all that determined. Weak-headed, I would say. WE, on the other hand, are very determined, and not at all angry. This is our night out on the town, and we won't be stopped by anybody. So we know: any attempt to return on your part would be . . . *inadvisable.*

MARGARET FOXXE (*shuns him*): It may be inadvisable to stay *here* any longer.

FROTH-BLOWER #2: She's right: let's get out of here before it's too late.

FROTH-BLOWER #1 (*avoiding the carpet*): Not so fast, Froth-Blowers, since we've only just arrived. [*To GEORGE FOXXE*]: What do you say, Mr Foxxe? [*Notices a stray straw on the table; picks it up; oggles it*]: Been drawing straws, eh? [*Turns*]: They've been drawing straws, comrades! [*Laughter from the group. FROTH-BLOWER #1 lights the straw with his cigar - and wooff! - it is gone.*]

ELAINE WICHELL: It is I who have something to say, sir.

JAMES BEAM: Here it comes . . .

[*The FROTH-BLOWERS all notice JAMES BEAM - and ROBERT GREENE - for the first time. The group murmurs that the two men, plus HORACE, represent no real challenge.*]

ELAINE WICHELL (*theateningly*): It is you, after all, who has drawn the shortest straw, sir.

[*The FROTH-BLOWERS focus on ELAINE WICHELL.*]

FROTH-BLOWER #1: I think, young Miss Ravenlocks, it's a longer straw than you realise. [*He gulps; he pops his eyes.*]

GEORGE FOXXE: For a while there, I thought we'd fallen into the hands of an unruly mob.

FROTH-BLOWER #1: I'm sorry to say this, Mr Foxxe, but you *have.*

[*He winks discretely at BARBARA, who pretends not to know him.*]

GEORGE FOXXE (*suspicious*): Friends of yours, Barbara? I hadn't realised.

BARBARA FOXXE: Guests of *ours*, George.

FROTH-BLOWER #1: And so we are, Mr Foxxe. We are the Ancient Order of Froth-Blowers.

GEORGE FOXXE: So you've already said. But how old is Ancient?

FROTH-BLOWER #1: Well, since you ask. Let's see now-.

GEORGE FOXXE: I heard you're outfit disbanded years ago.

FROTHBLOWER #2: We're still here, Mr Foxxe, as you can see. A reunion, call it.

[*Downstage, ROBERT GREENE slowly rises from the cubicle. He starts moving for the Stage L. portal.*]

FROTH-BLOWER #1 (*noticing*): You there: I don't recall saying anyone could leave.

[*ROBERT GREENE freezes; he hesitates, trying to decide whether to make a dash for the portal.*]

You there, with the sloping shoulders, I'm speaking to *you*. You're going to sneak off and abandon your friends at a time like this?

ROBERT GREENE: You're not talking to me, are you?

FROTH-BLOWER #1 (*angrily*): What are you implying? That I'm talking to myself? Why, I'll whip-.

[*ROBERT GREENE fixes the man's eyes.*]

FROTH-BLOWER #1: . . .You - I know you, don't I?

ROBERT GREENE: No, you don't.

FROTH-BLOWER #1: The cheek of it. [*To his colleagues*]: This
one's got to be a public servant. [*To R. GREENE*]: Now that
I think of it, your face is familiar - or is it just your sloping
shoulders. [*Commands*]: Now, be a good gentleman, and
return to your corner over there. Anyway, anyway - (*looks
upstage*) - you wouldn't desert your friends, would you?

FROTH-BLOWER #5: Sure he would.

FROTH-BLOWER #4: He looks the type who would desert
anybody at any time - anywhere.

FROTH-BLOWER #1: Anywhere but here, comrade. I won't have
it, you see? If there's one thing I can't stand, it's disloyalty,
even among the opposition.

ROBERT GREENE: I'm a guest here, passing though. I have no
friends here - is my guess.

FROTH-BLOWER #1: Well, if you don't have any friends, we'll be
your friends. Won't we, Froth-blowers? [*A cheer and a
whoop from the group.*] Now, don't make me angry. I don't
like being angry . . .

[*ROBERT GREENE complies.*]

That's what I like to see: a public servant that does as IT is
bid. . . [*Delighted*]: Now, I recognise you. [*Over his
shoulder*]: I'm blind to the obvious, comrades. This is one of
Errol Flynt's stooges. [*Upstage*]: Remember, comrades, they
came to us before the election. Then, after the election, we
were strangers to their fold.

GEORGE FOXXE: I should have known: the Mayor's been bought.

FROTHBLOWER #2: Bought and *sold*, Mr Foxxe! Bought and sold. [*All guffaw.*]

GEORGE FOXXE: And you fellows? I know you for what you are now.

FROTHBLOWER #2: In good time, Mr Foxxe. First, we have a certain public servant to deal with. We'll have us some sport, then hang him out to dry. A very public view for - Mr Greene, is it not - the PAMPHLETEER?

[*Excited*]: I heard, you know, that all the commotion outside was triggered by a single pamphlet. You'd have to be damned good to write a pamphlet like that - eh, what? Damned good.

[*All eyes turn to ROBERT GREENE.*]

Why, I saw a copy on the Strand - but when I picked it up, it was BLANK!

JAMES BEAM: Your conclusion, sir?

FROTH-BLOWER (*wipes the sweat from his brow*): My conclusion, my bearded friend, is this: a pamphlet that's blank - that has such an effect? Well, you can't get much better than *THAT*, CAN YOU?

[*ROBERT GREENE is re-seated. JAMES BEAM looks in that direction, is about to speak, but-.*]

MARGARET FOXXE: Why don't you leave the poor man alone? If he wants to leave, then why not let him leave?

FROTH-BLOWER #2: He can *try* and leave any time he wants, madam.

MARGARET FOXXE: That's not quite the same thing, is it?

FROTH-BLOWER #2: This, madam, is not a debating society.

MARGARET FOXXE: Oh really? Well, it's beginning to sound like one.

[*JAMES BEAM nods in agreement.*]

FROTH-BLOWER #1 (*not to be distracted*): You can discuss these fine points of etiquette on some other occasion. [*Chortles from the group.*] . . . It all comes down to the efficient use of assets in a deregulated marketplace, with an apparently liberalized tax regime, buoyed by a multitude of indirect taxes. You there, in the corner, Mr Greene, stick that in your alternative manifesto - and see that you and yours have no monopoly on political - or any other - virtue. If the people want socialism, then give them National Socialism. [*Over his shoulder*]: Now, I sound like a pamphleteer! [*Laughs.*]

GEORGE FOXXE: The efficient use of assets, you say? This sounds overly familiar.

FROTHBLOWER #1: It may sound familiar to you, Mr Foxxe; for us - it's a breakthrough! . . . The deal is done, Mr Foxxe. You there, with the beard: what do you say?

JAMES BEAM (*in analyitical mode*): The position is clear: the State is here to stay, but the private sector must pay for it. Who else is there?

FROTHBLOWER #1: Just so. If the government leaves us alone, then we'll leave the government alone. [*Confidentially*]: I've been considering the matter for some time now. . .As a collective, however, we Froth-Blowers are businessmen with an important mission to perform - *this* night.

GEORGE FOXXE: I thought you might be somehow. [*Defeated*]: You're with the Conglomerate, then? Which means. . .? - (*aghast*) - The Mayor is behind you-? Or you're behind the Mayor-?

[*In the cubicle, ROBERT GREENE recoils into the shadows.*]

JAMES BEAM: It's a travesty, George, of the system as we know - or don't know it.

FROTHBLOWER #1: Enough of that, greybeard. The *way* we perform the mission is up to us.

MARGARET FOXXE: I've never heard so much baloney.

GEORGE FOXXE: Please, Maggie, don't provoke them.

MARGARET FOXXE (*annoyed*): It is they who are provoking! You know how I detest secret societies, George! The Ancient Order of Blowers, indeed! Bah! Over-grown schoolboys is all.

FROTHBLOWER #2: That's *Froth*-Blower, madam. You mustn't leave out the Froth.

MARGARET FOXXE (*petulant*): The Ancient Order of Froth, then.

FROTH-BLOWER #1 (*over his shoulder*): You hear that, comrades? I do believe I detect ridicule.

MARGARET FOXXE: I detect b-.

GEORGE FOXXE: -That'll do, Maggie! [*To FROTH-BLOWER #1*]: She's had long day. An impossible day, as have well all. She doesn't know what she's talking about.

FROTH-BLOWER #1: I'll drink to that. [*He is passed an ale; he drinks, wipes his mouth with a swagger.*]

GEORGE FOXXE: She's confused you with the Elks, that's all. Or it is the Buffaloes? Her husband, anyway, was an Elk.

FROTH-BLOWER #2: Oh really, madam? A fine upstanding body of men, if I may say so.

[*MARGARET FOXXE dabs at her eyes with a handkerchief.*]

FROTH-BLOWER #3: Look what you've gone and done: you've made her cry.

FROTH-BLOWER #1 (*considers*): She's not crying . . .she's *laughing*! Curse the woman for her impudence. Why, if she weren't an elderly crone, I'd-.

GEORGE FOXXE: My friend, she could buy and sell you and your comrades a hundred-times over. Even *I* lay awake at night pondering that simple fact. So, I think you should allow the ladies to leave now - for your own sake, if not decency's.

FROTH-BLOWER #1: Think what you want, Mr Foxxe, but *no one* is allowed to leave. As for decency -.

MARGARET FOXXE (*recovering*): Why ever . . . not?

FROTH-BLOWER #3 (*leans forward from the snug*): Why, ah. Let me see. Yes. Club rules! No one is allowed to leave while the Ancient Order of Froth Blowers is in session. [*Withdraws.*]

ELAINE WICHELL: But we're not members of your club.

GEORGE FOXXE: Well said, Miss Wichell.

FROTH-BLOWER #1: Well said, but dead wrong. You have a problem with that, Mr Foxxe?

GEORGE FOXXE: If I had, would it matter?

> [*HORACE removes his coat and slings it to one side. After a lifetime of shifting barrels, he is muscle-bound. FROTHBLOWERS #3, #4 and #5 keep their eyes fixed on him.*]

FROTH-BLOWER #2 (*into the ear of #1*): The dumb waiter's on the move.

MARGARET FOXXE: You hear that, Elaine? Nothing but a rabble. They're worse than those thugs on the riverboat. There's only a difference of style. But not by much.

FROTH-BLOWER #1 (*worried*): Thugs? Which thugs might those be-?

GEORGE FOXXE: We had a little trouble down by the river earlier. An unexpected boarding party. The fellow you call the dumb waiter dispatched all of them. . . Single-handed.

FROTH-BLOWER #2: That fellow there - the mute?

FROTH-BLOWER #4: As a matter of interest, how many of them were there?

GEORGE FOXXE: Oh, about fifteen or so. I don't recall exactly how many. [*Pauses*]: There only seems to be *five* of you.

FROTH-BLOWER #2 (*looks over the snug*): Seems like a harmless enough fellow to me. . .

[*FROTH-BLOWER #1 glances at BARBARA; she nods very discreetly that the story is true.*]

GEORGE FOXXE (*noticing*): I ask again: Friends of yours, Barbara?

BARBARA: Guests of *ours*, George, darling.

FROTH-BLOWER #1: And, for now, we *are*: the Ancient Order of Froth-blowers. WE salute you, Mr Foxxe, in the only way we know how.

[*BARBARA is distracted - her allies retreat: FROTH-BLOWER #1 is passed a beer-glass by a comrade. The whole group, moving upstage in well-rehearsed concert, line up along the crimson carpet. Glasses raised, they perform a quick-blow of froth - which blasts around the place - and then drain their beers.*

It is only now that FROTH-BLOWER #1 looks down at his feet, and realises he is standing on the carpet. In fast succession - L.-to R. - the other Froth-Blowers become]

> *aware of their predicament. Downstage, HORACE is putting*
> *his coat back on - the confrontation (as far as he's*
> *concerned) is over.*
>
> *The carpet starts to move, and the five FROTH-BLOWERS -*
> *holding empty glasses over their heads - are transported*
> *towards the Stage L. portal. Behind the snug, HORACE*
> *appears to be cranking at something.]*

GEORGE FOXXE: So, you're glasses are empty, gentlemen, and you must be on your way. Thank you, for dropping by, and DON'T call again soon. [*Laughs; shakes JAMES BEAM's hand.*]

BARBARA (*stands up from barstool*): This can't be right! It's - impossible!

GEORGE FOXXE: You're right, Barbara, it never was right. What potions you have used on me, I do not know, but you kept me in my room for - three days and nights, was it? - and fed me visions of hell, then told me I was sick. But it was you, my dear, I was sick of.   Mistress, wife or housekeeper - whatever - you are neither of these things to me now, not that you ever were!

> [*FROTH-BLOWER #5 reaches out and grabs BARBARA by*
> *the wrist, so that she - too - is dragged onto the carpet, and*
> *transported away.*]

BARBARA (*on the move*): A windbag. You're a silly old man, George, whose time has passed. WE will succeed in the end. The efficient use of assets cannot be left to your kind any more.

GEORGE FOXXE: Not even if I own these same assets?

BARBARA: Not you, WE, the Co-. [*Her voice is lost.*] You signed, you old fool, you SIGNED your life away!

GEORGE FOXXE: The-? I did? She speaks, but there are no words, and even less meaning. At last, it is over. The medication was bad enough, but listening to her was worse. All's fair in love and war, they say, but I don't believe it - I never did. Well, take your Froth-Blowers, my love, and GO TO HELL!

[*BARBARA gesticulates with a scolding, but her voice speaks - without sound - into a partial vacuum . . .One-by-one, the five FROTH-BLOWERS and BARBARA disappear through the Stage L. portal. A perfect silence ensues. No one remaining wants to pass remark. Outside, the sky is black, and there is still no sign of St Paul's. HORACE carries on working behind the snug bar.*]

Horace? [*Turns his wheelchair slightly towards Stage R.*] Do you know anything about any of this? Horace, put that down, and answer me.

HORACE: Yes, Mr Foxxe?

GEORGE FOXXE: Do you know anything about this, Horace? What did I sign?

HORACE: I don't know, Mr Foxxe.

JAMES BEAM: You were hardly in a fit state to sign anything, George. A ruse, is my guess.

GEORGE FOXXE (*to HORACE*): Are you sure? You were alone on the Mikhail B. with her for quite a while, were you not?

HORACE: She was in the galley most of time. I was abovedecks.

GEORGE FOXXE: All right, Horace, all right. You'd better check that line again.

HORACE (*checks the 'phone*): . . .It's still dead, Mr Foxxe.

GEORGE FOXXE: Any voices in your head this time?

HORACE: No, sir.

GEORGE FOXXE: Well, that's something. We can't have you going crazy on us at a time like this, understand?

HORACE: I understand, sir.

GEORGE FOXXE: If the only voice in your head was Barbara's, I don't expect you to admit it; but if she was working on me, then she must have been working on you, too. I know, I know. What did she offer you?   Promotion? Preference shares in the new operation? Herself, perhaps-?

HORACE: If she offered me anything, sir, I'm not sure what it was.

GEORGE FOXXE: We'll make a diplomat of you yet, Horace. All right, then. She started it, and those fellows were brought in to finish it. Covert agents of some kind, she more than they . . . Wife? She was no wife to me. If I were married, I would know it, wouldn't I? Yes? No? You hear that, Maggie, I'm not married at all.

[*MARGARET FOXXE is pleased, but doubtful. HORACE, confounded, continues clearing up.*]

She was naught but a commercial whore. Brought in for the job.

JAMES BEAM: What kind of troop were they, anyway?

GEORGE FOXXE: Storm-troopers for the Conglomerate, though IT won't be so easily dispatched . . .Friends of Barbara, for sure, Jim. I'd say their next stop is Puddle Dock - whoever they are. By my recollection, the Ancient Order of Froth Blowers disbanded years ago. Imposters, from start to finish, though they'll wish they'd never set foot in The Arms this night. Know anything about this, Mr Greene? They seemed to know you - as a pamphleteer. Am I right?

ROBERT GREENE: I'm not sure that I do, Mr Foxxe.

JAMES BEAM: They seemed to know you Mayor Flynt, too.

ROBERT GREENE: Everyone, it seems, knows Errol Flynt.

ELAINE WICHELL: We're all imposters, until-. [*To GEORGE FOXXE*]: Until we're unmasked, and even then-?

GEORGE FOXXE: You have something rational to say, Miss Wichell? If so, I'd like to hear it.

ELAINE WICHELL: Those men were not what they seem - and nor is a member of *this* group.

GEORGE FOXXE: I don't mind saying so, Miss Wichell: but you've lost me - again

MARGARET FOXXE: Elaine, we'd better retire to our rooms. George? You have rooms at our disposal?

GEORGE FOXXE: I have a hundred rooms, Maggie. You can have Barbara's room, if you like - since she won't need that treacherous chamber any more. But, first, I want to hear what Miss Wichell has to say.

ELAINE WICHELL: The Professor knows - or suspects he knows - but he won't say.

GEORGE FOXXE (*sighs*): Is that right, Jim? You know something? Or suspect you know something?

ELAINE WICHELL: He's not saying, because he's not what he seems, either.

MARGARET FOXXE: Or you, Elaine. So, please, let us go - before something else happens.

[*ELAINE WICHELL observes ROBERT GREENE with interest.*]

ROBERT GREENE: You have something you want to say to me, Miss Wichell? If not, then I do believe I'll be on my way. [*Is about to stand.*]

ELAINE WICHELL: I recognise him now. [*All heads turn to look at her.*] At first, I thought it was an incubus or a succubus-.

ROBERT GREENE: What is she talking about?

MARGARET FOXXE: Elaine, please, you're embarrassing the other guests.

GEORGE FOXXE: The guests are beyond embarrassment, Maggie.

ELAINE WICHELL: And then I thought it was a resemblance, or that I was plain mistaken to have crossed such a great ocean, then to see the same man again: there on the riverboat, but under those chinese lanterns it was hard to tell exactly . . . But now -. There was a clue: evil shows its colour, but not its face - until now. It's green - in a blue suit. Look, everyone, you may never get another chance. Sightings are very rare. Down in Devon, over one-hundred and fify years ago. It was Christmas. Footprints over snowy ground. Up walls. Over roof-tops, across fields - a considerable distance - in no time at all!

ROBERT GREENE: She's flipped, finally.

MARGARET FOXXE: What are you talking about, Elaine? You're not having one of your turns, are you?

ELAINE WICHELL: On no, no. There's something coming from the East - at this very moment - but I don't know what it could be. . .I've been trying to ignore it, but - it's here.

ROBERT GREENE: You see? She's out of her skull.

ELAINE WICHELL: There are five of them, I think. Or six.

MARGARET FOXXE: But the Froth-Blowers have been and gone.

ELAINE WICHELL: - I don't have much time remaining, so - so here it goes. [*To MARGARET FOXXE*]: You remember, Margaret, what happened in New York last year?

MARGARET FOXXE: How could I forget?

ELAINE WICHELL: But you never *saw*, Margaret. You never *see*.

MARGARET FOXXE: Really, Elaine-! You cannot expect me to see what you *persistently* see!

ELAINE WICHELL (*speaks downstage*): But I saw you, Mr Greene. I saw you *there*. In New York

ROBERT GREENE: I can assure you, Miss Wichell, you saw me *nowhere*!

ELAINE WICHELL: But I saw you, Mr Greene, you were being questioned by-.

[*GEORGE FOXXE swivels his wheelchair to take a look at ROBERT GREENE.*]

ROBERT GREENE: I'm sorry, Miss Wichell, but that cannot be so. I was in New York last year, it's true. As part of a delegation to see your Mayor Gambini.

ELAINE WICHELL: If not, then I saw your double. Do you have a double, Mr Greene?

ROBERT GREENE: Yes, that must be it. It's possible. [*Unconvincingly*]: I've heard of such things. A doppelgänger? We'll have dinner some time, you and I, Miss Wichell - and discuss the matter further. But not now. [*Menancingly*]: Later .

ELAINE WICHELL (*upstage*): It was in Times Square. A riot was in progress. The demonstrators were dispersed. A lot of people were arrested that day. [*Impishly*]: Including me. The police, I thought, were kind of heavy handed - but not with you. [*Mocks*]: A proper English gentleman; a member of the delegation.

MARGARET FOXXE: Whom are you talking to, Elaine?

ELAINE WICHELL (*stands, moves upstage*): So, anyway, it was
the hottest of days. On the streets, the water hydrants gushed
like fountains under the sun. Children played and laughed. I
laughed. And then it started. The anger, the crush of bodies,
the smashing of glass. All that hate, where does it come
from, really? And then came the horses, and the batons, and
the gas. Phew! So the crowd panicked: no more hate, only
fear. You could taste it - yuk! And then - just like that - it
was a summer's day again. And it was all over. . .the
sidewalk. Red, sticky. So, before I was arrested, I witnessed
a strange encounter. There on the sidewalk, a couple of
policemen had detained an Englishmen. In New York, an
English accent carries on the wind: it's the last thing you
expect to hear in a situation like that, which was far from
polite. So, there we all were. I have this in-built curiosity -
part of the job, I suppose - and I listened, and then I looked,
and there *he* was. Dressed in an electric blue suit. An
innocent abroad. I looked his way, and then - I fainted. Only
for a few seconds, and when I opened my eyes - he had gone.

[*Raises her eyebrows.*] Anyway, it was me they arrested for
being an *agent provocateur* - the mastermind behind the riot.
Conspiracy, they said.

[*Turns*]: So, you see, Mr Greene, when I stepped onto the
boat this evening, I thought I'd seen a ghost.

MARGARET FOXXE: So what's new about that, Elaine? Are you
sure about all of this? Are you *quite* sure?

ELAINE WICHELL: Oh. He's gone. I frightened him away.

[*ROBERT GREENE has disappeared.*]

ELAINE WICHELL: You knew, Professor. You knew.

GEORGE FOXXE: Is this true, Jim?

JAMES BEAM: I'm associated indirectly with Mayor Gambini's
Office. As part of my special field assignment. I did not
know. I suspected. We knew our man would show his face in

London. We did not know that our man would turn out to be the Deputy-Deputy Mayor. Now, with Miss Wichell as witness. . .

GEORGE FOXXE (*incredulous*): You think she's a reliable witness?

JAMES BEAM: So long as she didn't imagine the whole thing, she'll make a perfect witness.

MARGARET FOXXE: There are always those two police officers.

JAMES BEAM: I'll find them, Mrs Foxxe. If they're still alive, that is, and not floating in the Hudson River - like our fellow guests Rose and Hatton float in the Thames.

ELAINE WICHELL: Water and fire, Professor - it's all inter-connected.

MAGARET FOXXE: That's quite enough of that, Elaine.

GEORGE FOXXE: You're under-cover, then?

JAMES BEAM: I *was* under-cover - until Miss Wichell'ds attennae started to twitch.

ELAINE WICHELL: Sorry about that, Professor.

MARGARET FOXXE: It is 'Professor', isn't it?

JAMES BEAM: You're welcome at my faculty any time, Mrs Foxxe.

MARGARET FOXXE: You may call me Margaret, Professor.

[*They exchange smiles. The word "Bequest", however, is in the Professor's eyes. In the downstage distance, the dome of St. Paul's gradually reappears.*]

GEORGE FOXXE: All right, that's enough of that. It may have escaped your attention, Professor, but your pigeon has flown its coop.

[A *massive, grey-white cloud forms in the downstage distance, then expands with Brownian movement towards The Arms, and engulfs the building.*]

ELAINE WICHELL: Ahhhhh. My voyage: time to embark.

[*The action freezes, except for ELAINE WICHELL, who turns to face Stage L. At the portal, the red-blazered MR SHINE appears. His tour group is huddled silently behind him.*]

Is that you, Mr Shine?

MR SHINE (*speaks in an underwater voice*): Is that you, Miss Wichell?

MISS WICHELL: It is me, but - oh! - where has everybody gone? [*Looks at where MARGARET FOXXE is sitting, then at the lounge, but to her eyes the place has been deserted. Outside, there is an opaque white mist.*] I'm supposed to be a witness, and I can't see a thing! They must have left without me!

MR SHINE: Why, everybody is here - with me - waiting for you. There's not much time left, Miss Wichell, so hurry along, if you will. The next tour starts in five minutes.

ELAINE WICHELL (*steps onto the carpet, turns, faces upstage*): Yes, I saw your group down by the river, earlier - but I just missed you. [*The carpet starts to move, conveying ELAINE WICHELL towards Stage L.*]

MR SHINE: Yes, yes, now let us be - on our way!

ELAINE WICHELL: This is wonderful! [*Wraps her arms about herself.*] But, but - my luggage - I left my luggage at the Savoy!

MR SHINE (*smiles in a sinister way*): You won't need any luggage where you're going, Miss Wichell!

[*ELAINE WICHELL arrives at Stage L. Then she, MR SHINE, and the rest of the group move gracefully and disappear through the portal. . . The scene in the lounge unfreezes. Outside, the opaque white mist turns to black night.*]

MARGARET FOXXE (*noticing*): Elaine!

GEORGE FOXXE: What is it now, Maggie?

MARGARET FOXXE (*stands*): It's Elaine - she's disappeared!

GEORGE FOXXE: I doubt very much if she's physically disappeared.

MARGARET FOXXE (*moving to Stage R.*): You underestimate her. [*Peers into the archway void at extreme Stage R.*]

GEORGE FOXXE: I underestimate everybody: that's how I earn my living, sister.

MARGARET FOXXE (*approaches the snug bar*): Horace, did Miss Wichell pass this way?

HORACE: I don't know, Mrs Foxxe.

MARGARET FOXXE: What do you mean you don't know?

HORACE: I was distracted.

MARGARET FOXXE: Distracted? By what?

HORACE: I don't know what it was.

GEORGE FOXXE: She's probably sneaked off to bed.

MARGARET FOXXE: Well, then I'll have to find her. Which room would she be in, brother?

GEORGE FOXXE: I have no idea. Any of the hundred.

MARGARET FOXXE: Then, I'll have to search all the rooms. I'll
see you in the morning, gentlemen, or at dawn, whichever
comes first. [*Bows her head, withdraws Stage R. into
archway void*].

GEORGE FOXXE (*to the archway void*): That could take some
time, Maggie. By the way, leave the Camerons alone. And
you'll find the light-switch there in the stairw-!

[*Stage lights to complete darkness.*]

She found it, all right.

[*A few silent moments pass in the darkness.   A yellow
spotlight appears at Centre- Stage, where HORACE stands
alone - his torso only visible - as he looks upstage, slowly
polishing a beerglass with a white cloth. The spotlight
changes, and slowly alternates between blue and red.*]

ROBERT GREENE (*unseen, but close-by*): Horace . . .? Horace?

HORACE (*looks up, startled*): Yes, sir? Is that you, Mr Greene?

ROBERT GREENE (*his head appears behind HORACE's left
shoulder*): What was all that? The carpet. And those Froth-
Blowers? What sort of place is this!?

HORACE: You may have chosen the wrong place to base your
operation, Mr Greene. As conspirators go, I think you'll find
yourself a beginner at The Arms.

ROBERT GREENE: Conspirator?

HORACE: The lawyer and the merchant banker: get in the way, did
they, sir?

ROBERT GREENE: And the Conglomerate? Who is the
Conglomerate?

HORACE: As far as I know, the Conglomerate is not a who, but an IT. IT seeks out assets, and then exploits them. Their methods are. . .questionable. You ought to know, sir; they financed the campaign last month.

ROBERT GREENE: Mayor Flynt's campaign? It was perfectly lawful fund-raising activity . . .but those Froth-Blowers, what do they want?

HORACE: A return on their investment is my guess, sir [*Polishes glass; it sparkles like a gemstone.*]

ROBERT GREENE: A little out of your depth, aren't you, Horace?

HORACE: Who, me, sir?

ROBERT GREENE: Why don't you take a stand, Horace?

HORACE: I've been standing up all day, sir.

ROBERT GREENE: Why don't you stand up for your class?

HORACE: I *am* standing up with my glass.

ROBERT GREENE (*appears at HORACE's right shoulder*): Those are your people out there, Horace.

HORACE: My people? I don't think so, Mr Greene.

[*ROBERT GREENE's head disappears.*]

JAMES BEAM (*unseen*): This whole thing's a cover up.

GEORGE FOXXE (*unseen*): We don't have cover-ups in this country, Jim. We have Government Inquiries.

[*ROBERT GREENE's head reappears at HORACE's left shoulder.*]

HORACE: You again, sir?

ROBERT GREENE: I was lost there, for a moment. There are some dark recesses in this place. . .

HORACE: Anything else, Mr Greene? I have duties.

ROBERT GREENE: Those were my lads on the boat; you hurt them bad; more than that, you frightened them. You have a certain technique . . .with your barge-pole . . .and (*reaches into HORACE's jerkin; pulls out a box of matches*) . . .these. [*HORACE stops polishing the glass; stares at ROBERT Greene's hand.*] You don't smoke, but you make fire. [*Replaces matches.*] Why?

HORACE: Stock in trade: in case someone asks me for a light, sir.

ROBERT GREENE: We could use a man like you, Horace. Join us. One day, I'll be Mayor. I need loyal footsoldiers.

[*ROBERT GREENE's head disappears; and reappears at HORACE's right shoulder.*]

HORACE: The goon-squad, sir? [*High-handedly*]: I think not.

ROBERT GREENE: You want to spend the rest of your days here - polishing glasses for the bourgeoisie. Tell me why?

HORACE: Your mind is poisoned with hate for them, Mr Greene. That's why. The bourgeoisie? The plutocracy? Whatever you like to call them.

ROBERT GREENE: As a class, I do. Don't you?

HORACE: No, sir: I've always felt sorry for them

ROBERT GREENE (*incredulous*): How can you feel sorry for them, Horace? Why?

HORACE: Well, sir, they need so much to get by on, don't they? . . .They must be very, very, very insecure people, sir, that's all I can say.

[*ROBERT GREENE blanches; he takes a step back, disappears into the shadows and reemerges, shorter by half-a-head, at HORACE's left shoulder.*]

ROBERT GREENE: You're plain old Horace Baker, what would you know about such things?

HORACE: I wasn't always a Baker, Mr Greene. The name was changed from Bakunin. My great, great, grandfather was Mikhail Bakunin.

ROBERT GREENE: You - a Bakunin? I don't believe it.

HORACE: I told you, sir - you're just a beginner around here.

ROBERT GREENE: Why, this is incredible. He was a revolutionary! In your heart, so are you. You're one of us, then!

HORACE: No, Mr Greene, I am not one of you. These days, I accept what is: inequality drives the system. Everything else is platitude.

ROBERT GREENE: Sometimes, Horace, you don't sound much like a bartender.

HORACE: I've been doing some reading. On the boat, sir. There's a lot of books on the boat. . .Where you're going, Mr Greene, you'll have time for plenty of reading, too - or writing pamphlets. On Dartmoor, say.

ROBERT GREENE (*enlightened*): All right, so you know my story, but I know yours. The cabin boy that came with the boat from Russia - the Mikhail B. I've got it now. I noticed your interest in pyrotechnics earlier on. You lived on the boat, but Mr Foxxe wanted you to live at The Arms. So you burnt down The Arms, and burnt up his wife. As a boy, you ran back to the boat, and that's when you found your secret corridor from here to the river; the same route we used this very night to escape the boat and return to The Arms.

HORACE: That was an accident. You're mistaken, sir.

ROBERT GREENE: Am I? It was an impossible event to live with - so you wiped it from your memory. [*Grins*]: I don't blame you.

HORACE: I did have a knock on the head this evening, sir, as you know. You're angry with me, sir, I understand that - but really, I don't think I can help you.

ROBERT GREENE: Old man Foxxe hasn't got a bloody clue, has he? If only he knew how his faithful retainer rewarded his hospitality. Tell me, Horace, where do you live now?

HORACE (*a lump in his throat*): On the boat.

ROBERT GREENE: On the boat, of course. Your home. A little piece of mother Russia on the Thames. You wouldn't leave it even if your life depended on it, would you, Horace? I'll wager that boat's library contains every book on combustion ever written. I know an obsessive streak when I see one. Pyromania? I have a special interest in that subject myself.

[*HORACE does not reply.*]

In our way, Horace, I think you and I have reached an understanding.

HORACE: A, sir?

ROBERT GREENE: An understanding. I can rely on your discretion, then?

HORACE: At The Arms, Mr Greene, we are the *soul* of discretion. As for any denunciation, I'll leave that kind of thing to you and yours.

[*ROBERT GREENE recoils, vanishes. . .The spotlight expands, showing GEORGE FOXXE and JAMES BEAM in private conversation.*]

GEORGE FOXXE: Horace, where have you been? Why are you standing there?

HORACE: Extra glasses for the party, sir.

GEORGE FOXXE: One extra glass, Horace? Having the party on your own?

HORACE: Quite right, Mr Foxxe; I'll locate some more. [*Removes himself to a position behind the snug bar, where he starts setting out ranks of champagne glasses.*]

JAMES BEAM: So you see, George, vanity always shows its face. Always.

[*Cut first spotlight. Stage lights gradually return. Enter ROBERT GREENE Stage L. portal - who is dazzled by a fresh, white spotlight . . .At Stage R., enter ERROL FLYNT with two DETECTIVES.*]

GEORGE FOXXE: Welcome, Mr Mayor, to The Arms.

ERROL FLYNT: Greetings, Mr Foxxe; Professor. I have an announcement to make, so I won't detain you for long.

GEORGE FOXXE: About time, too. Go ahead, Mr Mayor.

[*The two detectives cross the stage and apprehend ROBERT GREENE. They force their captive to look upstage - so that ROBERT GREENE stays dazzled . . .*]

ERROL FLYNT: Your promotion has just come through, Bob. I've come directly from the Assembly to tell you in person. Met the new Deputy-Deputy Mayor? She'll be here soon.

ROBERT GREENE: Get on with it, Errol.

ERROL FLYNT: There's a catch, Bob.

ROBERT GREENE: With you, there always is.

ERROL FLYNT: You won't able to take up your appointment for, say, twenty years or so.

ROBERT GREENE: Tell them about the Conglomerate, Errol. The Frothblowers - you sent them!

ERROL FLYNT (*upstage*): The poor man's become unreasonable.

ROBERT GREENE: If I stand trial, I'll bring you down with me!

ERROL FLYNT: You'll stand trial, all right, Bob. But not in London - in New York, where a man called Gambini is waiting for you. Take him away, gentlemen! Professor, a word if you please.

> [*The two DETECTIVES escort R. GREENE to Stage R. Cut spotlight. JAMES BEAM stands, and crosses the stage to join ERROL FLYNT, who shows his election-winning smile upstage. In the distance, there is applause.*]

GEORGE FOXXE: Anything else we can help you with, Mr Mayor? A contribution to campaign funds, perhaps?

ERROL FLYNT (*naked without his cronies*): Very generous of you, Mr Foxxe, but I was re-elected last week - as you know. The next election is in five years. If you'd like to contribute to-.

GEORGE FOXXE: I don't think so. [*To the snug.*] You hear that, Horace? Professor? Enough is never enough.

ERROL FLYNT: Professor Beam, I was hoping to discuss the extradition proceedings with you before-.

GEORGE FOXXE: - You hear me, young Flynt? There'll be an election, all right, but you won't be running. If your father knew, he'd be ashamed. If for one moment I suspected you were behind these Frother-blowers, I don't know what I'd say or do. Enjoy *this* term of office, Mr Mayor, but - after that - no more.

ERROL FLYNT: I think you've said enough, Mr Foxxe. I hear you loud and clear. [*Smiles upstage, waves. Exit ERROL FLYNT and JAMES BEAM.*]

[*HORACE re-emerges from behind the snug bar and joins GEORGE FOXXE.*]

GEORGE FOXXE: You and me, Horace.

HORACE: It certainly looks that way, sir.

GEORGE FOXXE (*pauses*): Horace, I'd like to look outside. [*HORACE swivels the wheelchair so that it faces downstage.*]

London's burning, Horace. I never thought I'd live to see the day. [*Ponders.*] It must have been something very like this during the Great Fire. What year was that again?

HORACE: I'm not sure I'd like to say, sir.

GEORGE FOXXE: You know but you won't say. Superstitious fellow, aren't you? The date? All the Sixes, but One. . .Then there was the Blitz. My own father was a boy then. The devil walked the earth that night, too.

HORACE: The devil doesn't exist officially any more, sir.

GEORGE FOXXE: Oh *sure.*

So, here we are now, on the edge of this inferno. I look, but I cannot bear the sight of it any longer.

[*HORACE promptly turns the wheelchair again, so that it is faces upstage. GEORGE FOXXE has tears in his eyes.*]

GEORGE FOXXE: . . .Horace, from now on, I think you'd better come and live here at The Arms. That would make me feel a whole lot better. [*Raises himself up, and stands out of the wheelchair - a tall, distinguished gentleman. For the first time, HORACE look surprised by events. GEORGE FOXXE raises an extinguished cigar to his lips.*]

Light me up, will you, Horace?

HORACE: I haven't got a light, sir.

GEORGE FOXXE: Yes, you have; there - in your jerkin.

[*HORACE strikes a light for the cigar, then snuffs it out between a thumb and finger. In between puffs, GEORGE FOXXE glances - for a second only - with a degree of suspicion at HORACE.*]

HORACE: Do you think we should have the carpet cleaned, Mr Foxxe.

GEORGE FOXXE (*puff-puffs cigar*): . . .It's in a hell of a state, Horace, it's true. But it's the dirt that holds it together. This old carpet will be around long after you and I have gone. Then again-.

[*The two men stare at the carpet, and - with their eyes - follow the runner all the way to the Stage R. portal. Enter PHYLLIS and JEFFREY CAMERON.*]

PHYLLIS CAMERON: Did we miss anything, Mr Foxxe?

[*By stealth, two thugs enter the Stage L. portal, and begin to roll up the carpet. They continue their work, uninterrupted.*]

GEORGE FOXXE: Not a thing, Mrs Cameron.

[*HORACE returns to his position at the snug bar. The CAMERONS join GEORGE FOXXE at Centre-Stage.*]

JEFFREY CAMERON: We fell asleep, Mr Foxxe.

GEORGE FOXXE (*glances at P. CAMERON*): I can well believe it, Mr Cameron. Please, join us. We embark on a new era this night.

PHYLLIS CAMERON: A new era of what, Mr Foxxe?

GEORGE FOXXE: I'm not sure, exactly, but we embark anyway. We have no choice

> [*The thugs have finished rolling up the carpet; they Exit Stage R. Demonstrators pour in from the Stage R. and Stage L. portal.*]

GEORGE FOXXE: Looks like we have company, Horace!

HORACE: Right you are, Mr Foxxe!

> [*Enter Stage R the RED-HEAD with her placard. The sign shows SWINE; she anchors it, and - with a marker - she crosses out the "S", and assists HORACE behind the bar.*
>
> *Enter, a COURIER with the promised case of champagne.*]

COURIER: Case of champagne for Mr Horace Baker! Courtesy of Trout Brothers Merchant Bank!

> [*HORACE and the RED-HEAD pour champagne into the ranks of glasses, then pass these among the guests.*
>
> *Enter Stage L. portal MERCHANT BANKER and the LAWYER - they are drenched from the river. They are given glasses.*
>
> *HORACE, the RED-HEAD and the COURIER work as a trio behind the snug bar.*
>
> *Enter Stage R., MARGARET FOXXE escorted by JAMES BEAM. They face upstage, take a bow, and join GEORGE FOXXE at Centre-Stage.*
>
> *Enter Stage L., CARLTON GREY - without his suit - but with a mangled shirt and Stars & Stripes jockey shorts. He bows, gracefully.*]

*Enter Stage R.   ERROL FLYNT and ROBERT GREENE -
both under close arrest between two DETECTIVES.*

*Enter Stage L., the riverboat boarding party of thugs. They
bow, like young gents.*

*Enter Stage. R., MR SHINE and his group, including
ELAINE   WICHELL   and   DR   SAXXE-COBURG,   EVA
FOXXE, MR STOKER and MISS ASHE.*

*Enter Stage. L, BARBARA escorted by THE ANCIENT
ORDER OF FROTH-BLOWERS. They bow, deeply.*

*GEORGE   FOXXE   signals   HORACE,   who   rings   what
appears to be the riverboat bell.*]

GEORGE FOXXE: Time, please, ladies and gentlemen - and the
rest of you!

[*The cast - with their glasses - salute upstage.*

[*Enter MISS PERKINS Stage R. with a facsimile sheet.*]

MISS PERKINS: The ID's come through from New York, Mr
Mayor! But- oh! It's a blue suit, all right, but - nobody's
inside it. Look - the head - it's a blank!

[*She moves Centre Stage to join ERROL FLYNT, the
DETECTIVES, and an elated ROBERT GREENE, who
appears to be dissolving.*

*Outside, the flames leap up into the sky. The Arms itself is on
fire. From the portal at Stage L, smoke creeps over the stage.
. .The RED-HEAD rotates her sign to show . . . "THE END?"*

*Lights shimmer, then dim, A spotlight appears at the Stage L.
portal. The WILD MAN, BAKUNIN enters, bearing a torch
of fire, more dishevelled than ever - and bounds to reach
Centre Stage. He bows, gracefully.*]

BAKUNIN: I was once a noble, you know - before I pursued the great cause. [*Looks L. - looks Stage R. - his eyes flashing.*] I am like a spark - a cinder - on the wind!

[*Stands upstage.*]

So, it has ended for now, my friends. Now, you may go out into the night - IF YOU DARE!

For beware: the city is no place for you, and nor is the COUNTRY!

[*Waves the torch before his eyes in a long, sweeping arc. Pauses, turns rapidly, and then takes a vaulting-run to Stage R., and dives through the archway void.*]

[*Exits. Silence.*]

[*The ensemble takes its final bow. The COURIER holds up a crumpled blue suit, devoid of its owner.*

CURTAIN.]

T H E   E N D

James A. Oliver
2001, 2004

CPSIA information can be obtained at www.ICGtesting.com
Printed in the USA
BVOW02s1929170316

440534BV00001B/19/P